THE SYNAPTIC GOSPEL

Teaching the Brain to Worship

Christopher D. Rodkey

University Press of America,® Inc.
Lanham · Boulder · New York · Toronto · Plymouth, UK

Copyright © 2012 by
University Press of America,® Inc.
4501 Forbes Boulevard
Suite 200
Lanham, Maryland 20706
UPA Acquisitions Department (301) 459-3366

Estover Road
Plymouth PL6 7PY
United Kingdom

All rights reserved
Printed in the United States of America
British Library Cataloging in Publication Information Available

Library of Congress Control Number: 2011941851
ISBN: 978-0-7618-5786-0 (paperback : alk. paper)
eISBN: 978-0-7618-5787-7

∞™ The paper used in this publication meets the minimum
requirements of American National Standard for Information
Sciences—Permanence of Paper for Printed Library Materials,
ANSI Z39.48-1992

Table of Contents

Acknowledgements and an Opening Apology	v
Chapter One Introduction, Problems, and Methodologies	1
Chapter Two Worshiping Communities as Circles of Empathy	13
Chapter Three The Neuroscience of Emotion and Feeling	27
Chapter Four The Neurology of Worship	49
Chapter Five Worship as Religious Education	63
Chapter Six An Ecology of Liturgy: Habituating Liturgically with Youth	73
Selected Bibliography	89
Index	93

Acknowledgements and an Opening Apology

It is impossible to fully acknowledge everyone I should as a means of giving thanks for their assistance. The seeds that began this project were instigated by Thandeka and Susann Pangerl. Early readers who advised this project and provided critical feedback include John Tolley, Neil Gerdes, Lisa Presley, Barbara ten Hove, Julia Argerter, and Russell Elleven. Others who have indirectly provided feedback to early stages of this project include Susan Harlow, W. David Arksey, Leslie Westbrook, Charles Courtney, and Thomas Magnell.

I also wish to acknowledge Thomas J. J. Altizer, who has been a theological mentor to me. This book is not so much an attempt to be a work of radical Christian theology as it is inspired by Altizer's radical understanding of the Kingdom of God. Clearly, a radical ecclesiology must fundamentally re-think the church as a whole, a task which is not my intention in this present work. However, a vision of the church that subversively inverses the contemporary trends of pastoral theology is indeed radical, and I hope that this book is a small step in this direction. Furthermore, although my intention in this present work is not to make an apology or translate radical Christianity for a broad audience, I believe that it is important to underscore that, for myself as a pastor and theologian, radical Christian theology is what emphasizes the absolute urgency of religious education for young people.

Others I must acknowledge: Candler School of Theology's Youth Theological Initiative; Princeton Theological Seminary's Institute for Youth Ministry; County College of Morris Library; Penn Central UCC Conference's Education Committee; and Lebanon Valley College's Religion and Philosophy Department. My pastoral work over this project began when I was a campus minister at DePaul University and briefly Pastor of Grace United Methodist Church, Blue Island, IL; continued while I was Youth Pastor of the Community UCC, Mountain Lakes, NJ; and currently, Pastor of Zion "Goshert's" United Church of Christ, Lebanon, PA. The youth, parents, and staff of the Community

UCC taught me youth ministry, but it was the larger congregation of this church who taught me the necessity and possibility of pan-generational worship. I would not have initially expected that the more mature, seasoned members of this congregation would have taught me more about youth ministry than the teens themselves—I wish to particularly acknowledge the Leef, Eveleth, Rajkumar, Meritt, and Dempsey families.

My close pastoral colleagues are essential to me for feedback and support. For this project in particular Josh Patty, Pastor of Central Christian Church, Fairmont, WV; and John Vest, Youth Pastor of Fourth Presbyterian Church, Chicago, IL, were very forthcoming and honest in their feedback. Other practitioners and conversation partners whose collegiality had an influence upon this book include Phil Blackwell, Diane Olson, Eugene Winkler, Phil Snider, Christina del Piero, F. Javier Orozco, Taylor Burton-Edwards, Jeffrey Robbins, the late Karen Calcagno, Chrissy Tippy, and Larry Kalp. Ms. Lyn Ridgeway of Chicago has been extraordinarily generous to my family, especially in hosting us in Chicago while working on this project. Many of my colleagues and friends on Facebook helped me select the subtitle for the book.

A few passages of this book were previously published; I thank the Order of Saint Luke, the Association of United Church Educators, and the Penn Central Conference of the United Church of Christ for supporting my writing ministry. Those articles appeared as "The Children's Sermon as Liturgical Movement" (*Education in the Church* [October, 2009], published online); "Reality Check" (*The Education Connection* [Winter, 2008]: 4+]; "A Polemic Against the Festival of the Christian Home" (*Sacramental Life* 17.2 [2005]: 18-23); and "Turning Away from Our Dead" (*Sacramental Life* 17.2 [2005]: 7-9).

I wish to thank my family, immediate and extended, and especially my spouse, Traci, who has been my primary support in completing this book and seeing it published. Our son, Christian, was born as I began writing *The Synaptic Gospel*, and the research stage for the book coincided with his advent. Now, as I have been preparing this book for a wider audience, I have been doing so in the presence of a new child, Annaliese. The exigency of rethinking how we raise children in the church is heightened for me by their coming into the world, as someone who sincerely believes that a peaceful and just future relies upon the strength of the emerging church latent within their hands, New Flesh of the resurrection.

An Apology

Finally, I wish to say a few words about the text itself. The book is organized into six chapters. The first chapter introduces the problems posed by the book and discusses methodology. Chapter two establishes my prioritization of empathy as a key element of a Christian worshiping community by way of an engagement with phenomenological philosophy. Chapters three and four explore the scientific aspects of emotion and feelings. The final two chapters bring all of the previous discussions together and offer a principle-based paradigm for pastoral ministry, and offer some examples.

I recognize that my primary audience for this book—pastors and religious education workers—generally do not have the theoretical training to necessarily walk directly into a philosophical or scientific discussion without significant preparation. I have attempted to write this book in such a way that the language would make sense to most pastors and religious educators, but at the same time I am constructing a scholarly argument that may be too specific for some of my readers.

That being said, I want to encourage my readers who may be intimidated by the technical aspects of this text to read confidently, but I also suggest that some readers may want to skip or skim chapters two through four, and then return to those chapters' arguments later. The final two chapters are the payoff for the practitioner; it is my hope that my fellow pastors and religious educators do not abandon my conversation because of the academic style of my writing or argumentation.

Christopher D. Rodkey
Lebanon, Pennsylvania
Feast of the Dormition of Saint Mary
August 15, 2011

Chapter One
Introduction, Problems and Methodologies

What could we learn if we applied the theories and knowledge of brain science to the language and theologies of Christian worship? In other words, what would a ministerial paradigm look like, if, as part of its normative assumptions, such a paradigm took a *neurologically-informed* approach to its task? These questions have implications for religious education: in particular, what role does brain development have in the fostering an inter-generational faith community? This latter question is particularly salient to a practice of youth ministry that seeks to address the complexities of adolescence, a period of time which is marked by a great deal of physiological changes. The practice of youth ministry, however, has only recently taken the neurological development of teens seriously. These are the questions that I seek to explore in *The Synaptic Gospel*.

Why a consideration of neuroscience and liturgical theology?[1] Clearly, our emotional experience of the world is an essential component of liturgical experience. Many of the debates surrounding the so-called "contemporary worship" surround the nature of emotions, or feelings—*affects*—in worship settings.* Our feelings, when evoked in worship, must be understood as not only a "spiritual" experience (however one might define *spiritual*), but also a

---

* Although the difference between *feeling* and *emotion* is not necessarily relevant to this project, I will use the term *emotion* as a discreet mental state and *feeling* as a more pervasive affective state. Emotions, on one hand, have a clear beginning and an end, while feelings *spill* beyond the mind and are complexly related—and interrelated—throughout the body.

physiological experience. By this I mean that our emotions are rooted in our bodies and specifically, our brains. Therefore, a consideration of how emotions occur would obviously facilitate a succinct discussion on how to think about worship.

My approach to this question, however, is not one that will necessarily lead to specific answers about the origin of religious experience. Scientists and psychologists cannot agree on exactly how emotions and feelings physiologically or chemically *happen*. To commit to one specific theory would make this study obsolete nearly immediately, as there is not only little agreement among the experts, but the *scientific* truth—if it is *ever* discovered—is quite likely *none* of the current theories! Regardless, a study of contemporary approaches will show some common agreement about how the brain develops, and how brain development is connected to memory, learning, and our human capacity for emotion and feeling. As such, a new (or perhaps *renewed*) theological paradigm for thinking about experiencing emotion and feeling within religious communities in public worship will arise.

I wish to be transparent about my theological bias, though I will discuss some of my liturgical backgrounds and experiences later. In approaching neurological theology I am clearly not a neuroscientist, but I attempt to make the science intelligible to my highly intelligent audience. I have included in the notes a bit more science for those seeking more information. I will often let the theorists speak for themselves, and then make my own conclusions; my use of longer quotations is intentional. Theologically and personally, my own theological thinking has been deeply influenced by Thomas J. J. Altizer's Christian theology; therefore, it follows that at bottom my primary ministerial concern is the Kingdom of God, that is, the possibility of living in community as a genuine people of God.[2] This bias will become more clear in the final chapter; however, one should be aware of my bias. To this end, I do not believe that this study assumes that my reader is theologically congruent or even compatible with my own specific doctrinal positions.

"Neuro-theology" and Methodology

I wish to be clear in my methodological approach. In recent years, a new field called "neuro-theology" has emerged. Generally speaking, neuro-theology seeks to make a scientifically-based argument for the existence of God, the human need for, or dependence upon, a God or the "idea" of God, based upon neurological science.[3] Some forms of neuro-theology argue, quite simply, for a biological necessity for religious experience, and theologically what arises from this line of thinking is often a syncretistic philosophical approach to the plurality of religions, given that all humans share the same neurological *form*.[4] Some neuro-theologians have even suggested—as I will later, but from a different methodological perspective—that new rituals be developed to reflect the theorists' biological assumptions for religious experience.[5]

I reject this methodology not only because of the lack of finality to the scientific bases which neuro-theologians use, but more importantly because I do not find an exigency in *proving* a necessity for the reality of God or for a scientific legitimacy of affective religious experience. One might say that I question, from my non-scientific point of view, *both* the science of neuro-theology's science *and* the theological motives of neuro-theology's theologies.[6] Clearly, whenever writing theologically or philosophically (or even *scientifically*) about emotions or feelings, one must be very careful not to make reductionist, colonialist, essentialist, universalizing, or even just *epistemologically pretentious* assumptions about human experience. Often what constitutes specific feelings and their meanings are culturally conditioned and shaped by the socio-political and economic contexts in which the individual lives.[7] I intend to be sensitive to this concern.

My methodology, conversely, is to employ the recent trends in neurological science to understand how emotions and feelings come about within humans, to facilitate a practical theological discussion. In some ways, this method is not distant from a theological *use* of natural philosophy or something that "resembles" natural philosophy.[8] In other words, the framework for my theological employment of neuroscience is a philosophical one, which is to say, I wish to *use* neuroscience as a tool to help disclose the phenomenon and content of the human experience of emotion and feeling.[9] This concern arises partially out of necessity, since, as John Corrigan points out, the historical-critical "study of religion has avoided engaging emotion" outside of pastoral or liturgical theology.[10] Aside from the Wesleyan notion of "heart-religion,"[11] that is, that Christian religious experience has at its root some kind of essential affective component, the most significant post-Reformation theological or philosophical discourse on the nature of emotion originated in the Scottish Enlightenment.[12] The Scottish philosopher Francis Hutcheson argued for a notion of *sensus communis*, that is, that we all have a "universal inclination" for others' feelings. Hutcheson's more famous student, David Hume, epistemologically advocated that human minds mirror one another in terms of their emotional content.[13]

Although other philosophers have written on this topic, in the twentieth century, phenomenological philosophers Edmund Husserl and Edith Stein (known to some as St. Theresa Benedicta of the Cross) revolutionized the meaning of "empathy." For Stein, in particular, empathy is the means by which we collect data about other people in the world, but empathy is also how we move beyond the data-collecting act to engaging in authentic relationship with others. Stein's conception of empathy, then, brings two individuals into a common, shared, religious experience by reflecting ourselves through another person as a means of self-knowing or self-actualizing. One cannot have a discussion of feeling and worship, let alone emotion and Christian ministry, without a discussion of empathy; as such, we will later explore empathy as it has come to us historically from the Continental philosophical tradition.

Turning to the subject of liturgical theology or worship, in terms of methodology, I understand ritual as not a specifically Christian practice, but an act through which I am interpreting from my own specific "mainline," Protestant Christian perspective. Although I am ecclesiastically an ordained member of the United Church of Christ—the Congregationalist tradition—I am a former member of evangelical Protestant and Wesleyan religious traditions, and I have been shaped in my formal religious education by Roman Catholic and Unitarian Universalist perspectives. (I assume that this hybridity is not necessarily an uncommon religious experience in the United States today.) That said, I recognize that ritual studies, as an academic discipline, has a great importance in linguistic studies, gender studies, psychoanalysis, and the history of religions, and acknowledge that my project is *not* squarely any of these, but I acknowledge the importance of these disciplines and their contributions.[14] I also want to be clear that I do not stand with an academic objectivity to the phenomenon of ritual: I believe that ritual can be a very negative, hurtful, and even *evil* experience.[15] On the other hand, I *do* make a value judgment regarding ritual: I *passionately* believe that ritual can be a positive, rewarding, liberating, regenerative, and even *redemptive* experience that is largely essential for religious communities to engage and connect to each other. As I hope to demonstrate, this discussion will *emphatically* lead, in its conclusions, to this assumptive passion.

Exactly *how* positive or negative affective experience operates within Christian worship has been a debate for centuries. Jonathan Edwards, who himself was one of the architects of an extremely successful, emotion-laden revival, wrote in the 1750s his *Thoughts on the Revival of Religion in New England*, a methodology for safely manipulating the affections of those in worship, so as not to be unethical or Satanic.[16] Yet the wide variety of emotions that individuals report to have experienced in Christian worship settings is astounding. One psychological study surveyed nuns and priests regarding which emotions they experience toward God, which include all of the following, in order of frequency: gratitude, hope, friendliness, happiness, reverence, affection, delight, enjoyment, inspiration, serenity, cheerfulness, confidence, admiration, determination, amusement, relief, pride, passion, solemnity, impatience, remorse, grief, guilt, irritation, anxiety, frustration, sadness, anger, fear, pity, shame, nervousness, depression, embarrassment, jealousy, apathy, panic, resentment, boredom, disgust, dislike, hate, and contempt![17] Clearly, there is no shortage of the wide variety of emotions that one might experience in worship settings. The current religious climate of the United States is also divided about the nature of emotion in worship.

THE CONTEXT:
CONTEMPORARY PROTESTANT WORSHIP

It is difficult at any time in history to speak of Protestant liturgical theology as a unified whole, since by "Protestant" one might include anything from Congregationalists to evangelical fundamentalists, from Moravians to Mormons, from Unitarian Universalists to Appalachian snake-handlers! Yet in the United States, given this multiplicity of theological traditions, current worship *trends* are more homogenized than one might expect. The influence of charismatic Pentecostal Protestantism in American Christianity, for example, has even influenced the *trends* of worship in Roman Catholicism, as well as Protestantism.[18] The phenomenon of television evangelism has changed the way in which many Americans think about technology outside of church, raised interesting questions about the corporate and isolated nature of public Christian worship, and even influenced evangelical Protestants' political visibility.[19] The rise and popularity of so-called "Contemporary Christian Music," or Christian popular culture, has created a revolution, as well as a multi-million dollar industry, in the way by which mainline Protestants now engage new technology and think about liturgical music, including a reclamation (for good or ill) of American Protestantism as a sung theology.[20]

One might characterize many of these *trends*—which are not denominational-specific, but *pan-denominational*—as directly engaging, or perhaps simply questioning, the legitimacy of the direct manipulation of emotion and feeling in worship settings. Some of the backlash against these trends, which are often "reductionistic" appeals to tradition or *orthodoxy* (literally, "right worship"), often surprisingly come from the more theologically-progressive or liberal factions of American denominations, who typically claim that these new trends place *too much* emphasis on emotion and feeling—to the point of claiming that such "new" worship experiences are emotionally *manipulative*—or that they move toward a *solipsistic* (that is, an extremely individualized) understanding of Christian worship and practice.[21] In other words, these trends promote an *individualized* and *self-centered* worship, rather than a *communal* and *corporate* experience.[22] One argument could be made from a more formal, oral language-driven liturgical perspective that an affective "*passion* for knowledge," which leads to an exploration of "higher things," is the appropriate affective nexus for Protestant worship.[23] Others have even argued that these "emotional" trends focus on too many of the so-called *positive* emotions, or are too "saccharine" in their worship experience; instead, the notion of the "fear" of God needs to be reclaimed in Protestant worship.[24] At bottom, a fundamental question concerning these trends, as well as what might constitute *legitimate* Christian worship, centers around emotion and its role in Protestant liturgy.

One new trend is the "emergent church" movement, which claims to rethink the Christian worship and communal experience from top to bottom.[25] This fairly recent trend—which is difficult to generalize and summarize—seems to focus its worship experiences, on one hand, upon being driven by a need for genuine emotional responses from the worshipper within what is often a very small community, and on the other, upon emphasizing adoration as a primary emotion to be experienced in worship.[26] In other words, the affective center of emergent worship should be driven by a love for God. Neuro-theological methodological tendencies, however, have not been absent from the "emergent" trend, with some emergent church theorists using neurological science to speculate a systems theory based around the physiology of the human nervous system as a fundamental metaphor for the new ways by which "emergent" church-goers think about their interconnectedness as a community.[27] Clearly, both the question of the relation of the affections and the possibility for the use of brain science in liturgical theology are latent within the current trends of Protestant worship; it is my intention that, as a matter of method, my research is not trend-specific but might inform the broad field of practice of Christian worship today.

PASTORAL CONCERN

This project does not arise only from a need to construe interesting questions or merely to be an academic exercise. Youth ministers and church youth workers today constantly work through the current trends of how best to worship with young people, but they also engage larger questions about how children and youth develop into adulthood—and how churches can enhance or hinder this experience. These concerns are usually relegated to the basements of small pastoral theology departments in seminaries, labeled as "religious education." The reality, however, is that for the majority of "mainline" Protestant churches, many of which are very small, the primary evangelism focus is placed upon raising youth within the faith.

Many of the worship trends that I mentioned earlier tend to be generational-specific—whether intentionally or unintentionally so. In other words, often a congregation will enact or offer a "Contemporary Christian Music" type of worship for the sole purpose of enticing or attracting certain age groups that are not present, or under-served by, the current worshipping community. These demographic groups are usually youth and young adults. While I generally do not have any cause to object to offering innovative, fresh, and even exciting new ways to worship and evangelize through worship, it seems to me that *such thinking operates with an axiom or basic assumption that different generations of people cannot worship together because they speak different liturgical and existential languages*. It is *potentially*, in essence, a *declared failure* of the biblical image of the "body of Christ," exemplified by the fact that different generations are simply unable to worship together (Ephesians 4:4: "There is one body and one Spirit").

While my judgment may or may not be true of every church participating in the newer trends of worship, this is embarrassingly true among more traditional, "mainline" Protestants of nearly every denomination. One practice, which is clearly indicative of my negative claim, is that of removing children and even teenagers during the regular Sunday morning worship hour in favor of Sunday School. This *bad habit* pontificates religious education to something that occurs outside of the worship space, performed by adults removed from the worship space, and even *at odds* with what goes on in the worship space.[28] A very recent trend is to simultaneously utilize separate worship spaces for varying age groups.

I will discuss this practice in more detail later; however, I mention it now to give a sense of the *exigency* for new liturgical thinking of ministerial practice in terms of neurological development. In church situations where children, and especially teens, are removed from the worship practices of the congregation, *neurologically speaking*, the children and youth are being *trained* or "habituated" by the congregation into a community experience which removes them from the older generations. It is no wonder so few teenagers return to Christian churches as adults: they have been *habituated* into having a social role where one goes to church to not really attend church. And even within this habituation, when and if they do return, finding communal *meaning* from symbols and liturgical language with which they are unfamiliar will only hinder their attachment and ability to find a shared experience with a congregation of people of varying ages.

PASTORAL THEOLOGY

Stepping backwards in time a bit, German Idealist philosopher and theologian Friedrich Schleiermacher made a clear connection between pastoral theology and emotion. In his *Practical Theology,* Schleiermacher writes that

> practical theology is defined as the *Teknik for maintaining and perfecting the church.* . . . By *Teknik* we refer to instruction about how to bring something about. . . . Practical theology should show us how these tasks must be carried out in order to reach their goal.

He clarifies further: "the task of practical theology is to bring the emotions arising in response to events in the church into the order called for by deliberate activity." There is, then, not *Teknik* "without emotion."[29] Feeling, or *Gefühl*, for Schleiermacher, critic Thandeka observes, "fills the human 'gap' between the rational mind and the empirical world (which includes the rational mind's body)." Emotion provides, as phenomenological philosophy would explore later, the way in which *I* relate to everything that is *not-me*, but for Schleiermacher, feeling is not only the sensation that arises from my experience of the world—that which is *not-me*—but also the means by which *I* might self-actualize and *reassert* my self.[30] Through emotion, I can learn to love, be aware of others, and be myself. To have the *courage to feel* is to have the *courage to be*.[31]

It is with this courageous sprit that I move into my exploration of neurological science and liturgical theology, that is, an *embodied* or *enfleshed* liturgical theology.[32] In this sense, I intend this project to clearly be a work of pastoral theology, and *not* one of neuroscience, psychology, or the so-called "neuro-theology." Perhaps a better fitting term is Affect Theology—that is, a theological discourse that arises out of a consideration (whether scientific or non-scientific) of *Gefühl*, feeling, as a primary human experience.[33] Regardless, it is my intention in this pastoral and academic enterprise to offer what I hope to be a new theological paradigm for thinking or re-thinking worship as a community that is the Body of Christ in a way that helps us find meaning in ourselves and a togetherness that is *liberating* and *regenerative* to a people seeking revitalization and restoration, and is pleasing to "God"—however defined or realized by individual faith communities themselves. To do so, I will argue, is to not only *think liturgically*, but to *live* liturgically: *living the Kingdom of God*, while remaining *embodied* in our *habituations*.

NOTES: CHAPTER ONE

1. Cf. Jaak Panksepp, *Affective Neuroscience* (Oxford: Oxford UP, 1998), 320.

2. For Thomas J. J. Altizer's most important works, see *The Gospel of Christian Atheism* (Philadelphia: Westminster, 1966); *The Descent Into Hell* (Philadelphia: Lippincott, 1970); *The Self-Embodiment of God* (New York: Harper & Row, 1977); *Total Presence* (New York: Seabury, 1979); *The New Gospel of Christian Atheism* (Aurora, CO: Davies, 2002); *Godhead and the Nothing* (Albany: SUNY UP, 2003); and *Living the Death of God* (Albany: SUNY UP, 2006).

3. Jonathan Feit, "Probing Neurotheology's Brain, or Critiquing an Emerging Quasi-Science," *The Council of Societies for the Study of Religion Bulletin* 33.1 (Feb. 2004), 3; cf. Andrew Newberg, Eugene d'Aquili, and Vince Rouse, *Why God Won't Go Away: Brain Science & The Biology of Belief* (New York: Ballantine, 2001), 46-53; Rollin McCraty and Doc Childre, "The Grateful Heart: The Psychophysiology of Appreciation," *The Psychology of Gratitude*, eds. Robert Emmons and Michael McCullough (New York: Oxford UP, 2004), 232ff.

4. Eugene d'Aquili and Andrew Newberg, *The Mystical Mind: Proving the Biology of Religious Experience* (Minneapolis: Fortress, 1999), 5, 12-13, 18; Michael Persinger, "The Temporal Lobe: The Biological Basis of the God Experience" in *NeuroTheology: Brain, Science, Spirituality, Religious Experience*, ed. R. Joseph (San Jose, CA: University Press, 2003), 273-278; Anthony Newberg and Jeremy Iverson, "On the 'Neuro' in Neurotheology" in *NeuroTheology: Brain, Science, Spirituality, Religious Experience*, ed. R. Joseph (San Jose, CA: University Press, 2003), 251-269; Lawrence

McKinney, *Neurotheology: Virtual Religion in the 21st Century* (Cambridge, MA: American Institute for Mindfulness, 1994).

5. As do Andrew Newberg and Eugene d'Aquili in d'Aquili Newberg (1999), 107.

6. Massimo Pigliucci, in "Neuro-Theology, A Rather Skeptical Perspective" (in *NeuroTheology: Brain, Science, Spirituality, Religious Experience*, ed. R. Joseph [San Jose, CA: University Press, 2003], 269), makes a similar argument.

7. Amélie Oksenberg Rorty, "Enough Already with the 'Theories of the Emotions,'" in *Thinking about Feeling: Contemporary Philosophers on Emotions*, ed. Robert Solomon (New York: Oxford UP, 2004), 278; cf. Thandeka, "Schleiermacher's *Affekt* Theology," *International Journal of Pastoral Theology* 9 (2005), 214; Robert Ornstein, *The Psychology of Consciousness* (San Francisco: Freeman, 1972), 119-120. Panksepp calls this kind of reductionistic thinking a "naturalistic fallacy" (Panksepp [1998], 320, 425 n. 89). I categorize the idea of "spiritual indexing" and the like into this brand of flawed approaches to pastoral theology (cf. Robert Darden, "Spiritual Assessment and Treatment Strategies," *The Remuda Review* 42 [2005], 15).

8. Patricia Churchland, *Brain-Wise: Studies in Neuro-Philosophy* (Cambridge, MA: MIT UP, 2002), 373. A similar methodology is proposed in Eric Kandel, "A New Intellectual Framework for Psychiatry," *American Journal of Psychiatry* 155.4 (April, 1998): 457-469; and *ibid.*, "Biology and the Future of Psychoanalysis: A New Intellectual Framework for Psychiatry Revisited," *American Journal of Psychiatry* 156.4 (April 1999): 505-524.

9. Cf. Thandeka (2005), 200.

10. John Corrigan, "Introduction: Emotion Research and the Academic Study of Religion," in *Religion and Emotion*, ed. John Corrigan (New York: Oxford UP, 2004), 5.

11. Cf. John Wesley, in John and Charles Wesley, *Selected Writings and Hymns*, ed. Frank Whaling (New York: Paulist), 106-107 ("Extracts from John Wesley's Jounal: 8th January to 24th May 1738," para. 12-16).

12. Thandeka (2005), 204-205.

13. Lydialyle Gibson, "Mirrored Emotion," *University of Chicago Magazine* 98.4 (April 2006), 39.

14. Delwin Brown, *Boundaries of our Habituation: Tradition and Theological Construction* (Albany, NY: SUNY UP, 1994), 97; cf. Thomas Oden, *Pastoral Theology: Essentials for Ministry* (Cambridge, MA: Harper, 1983), 203.

15. David Hogue, *Remembering the Future, Imagining the Past: Story, Ritual, and the Human Brain* (Cleveland: Pilgrim, 2003), 183ff.. Cf. Walter Freeman, "A Neurological Role of Music in Social Bonding," *The Origins of Music*, ed. Nils Wallin, Björn Merker, and Steven Brown (Cambridge, MA: MIT UP, 2000), 421; Mary Daly, *Gyn/Ecology: The Metaethics of Radical Feminism* (Boston: Beacon, 1978); cf. d'Aquili and Newberg (1999), 211.

16. Jonathan Edwards, *Thoughts on the Revival of Religion in New England, 1740* (New York: American Thought Society, 1845), 238ff.

17. Pamela Samuels and David Lester, "A Preliminary Investigation of Emotions Experienced Toward God by Catholic Nuns and Priests," *Psychology Reports* 56 (1985), 706.

18. Larry Eskridge, "Slain by the Music," *Christian Century* 123.5 (7. March 2006): 18-20.

19. Richard Wolff, "A Phenomenological Study of In-Church and Televised Worship," *Journal for the Scientific Study of Religion* 38.2 (1992): 219-235, esp. 233ff.

20. Contemporary Christian Music, or "CCM," is a phenomenon that I have dealt with in earlier academic and pastoral publications, to which I refer my reader: Christopher Rodkey, "Hymnody as Public Theology," *Sacramental Life* 15.1 (2002/2003): 451-458; *ibid.,* "The Practice of Music in Youth Ministry and the Mystery of the Divine," *Journal of Youth and Theology* 5.2 (2006): 47-62. See also Dan Lucarini, *Why I Left the Contemporary Christian Music Movement* (Webster, NY: Evangelical, 2002), 50-51, which discusses the "controversy" around the question, *what is the "heart" of worship?* Interestingly, this debate—which I find largely perplexing—is handicapped by the fact that the language of the "heart of worship" is vaguely described in popular CCM worship songs, which prevent a theological discussion from ever getting very far, as well as the ambiguity of the word "heart": does "heart" in our songs mean "center," "foundation," "nexus," etc., or does it mean *emotion* or *affect*? And what might it mean for affect to be the foundation of worship?

21. Thandeka (2005), 214. Cf. Mary Van Leeuwen, "Between Reductionism and Self-Deification: The Challenge of the Cognitive Revival," *Center Journal* 4.2 (Spring 1985): 39-69.

22. Wolff, 234; William Willimon, "It's Hard to be Seeker-Sensitive When You Work for Jesus," *Circuit Rider* 27.5 (September/October 2003), 5; Cf. Kenda Creasy Dean, "The Problem with Passion: Or, Why the Church of Mel Gibson is Doing Just Fine," in *The Princeton Lectures on Youth, Church, and Culture: 2004* by Kenda Dean et al (Princeton, NJ: Princeton Theological Seminary, 2004), 7-9.

23. Robert C. Roberts and W. Wood, "Proper Function, Emotion, and Virtues of the Intellect," *Faith and Philosophy* 21.1 (January 2004), 15.

24. Cf. Lucarini, 57-58.

25. Cf. Dan Kimball, *Emerging Worship: Creating Worship Gatherings for a New Generation* (Grand Rapids, MI: Zondervan, 2004), 9.

26. Rob Weber and Stacy Hood, *ReConnecting Worship: Where Tradition & Innovation Converge* (Nashville: Abingdon, 2004), 35-41, 75.

27. Chuck Smith, "What is Emerging?", *Worship Leader* 14.2 (March/April 2005), 24. I will note that my position is that such metaphors are both a misuse of neuro-theological trends and a mixed metaphor in its relations to systems theory. One criticism that arises from a cultural hegemonic discourse (which is often connected to a racist critique) is that such ecclesiological thinking that emphasizes this interconnected level of "intimacy" is ultimately bad, since it is ostensibly connected to that of sexual intimacy (Lucarini, 72-73).

28. I wish to be careful about this claim. The simultaneous church-religious education hour model can work for many churches; I am suggesting that, especially for small churches whose resources are limited, one should be *very careful* when doing this.

29. Friedrich Schleiermacher, *Christian Caring: Selections from Practical Theology*, trans. James Duke, ed. James Duke and Howard Stone (Philadelphia: Fortress, 1988), 98, 99-100.

30. Thandeka, *The Embodied Self: Friedrich Schleiermacher's Solution to Kant's Problem of the Empirical Self* (Albany, NY: SUNY UP, 1995), 2, 94ff.; cf. Friedrich Schleiermacher, *The Christian Faith*, 2nd German ed., ed. J. Mackintosh and J. Stewart (Edinburgh: T&T, 1952), 6ff.

31. Cf. Paul Tillich, *The Courage to Be* (New Haven, CT: Yale UP, 1952); Mary Daly, *Webster's First New Intergalactic Wickedary of the English Language* (Boston: Beacon, 1987), 69-70.

32. Thandeka (1995), 118; d'Aquili and Newberg (1999), 148; cf. Corrigan, 15-16.

33. Thandeka (2005), 205. According to Thandeka, Schleiermacher's understanding of the term *affect* is "the locus of the shift of immediate self consciousness;" in other words, *affect* "refers to a fundamental structural device within the human organism that carries the experience of personal coherence of the self, from an organic experience, from one determinate movement of consciousness to the next" (205). Following this, for Thandeka, *affect* is "the biological foundation of faith." This is so because "[e]very human experience is affective" (207). In thinking along these lines, I am also grateful to Walter Freeman's innovative methodological interplay between neuroscience and continental philosophy—as in his article, "Happiness Doesn't Come in Bottles: Neuroscientists Learn That Joy Comes Through Dancing, Not Drugs," *Journal of Consciousness Studies* 4.1 (1997): 67-70, especially on p. 69.

Chapter Two
Worshiping Communities as Circles of Empathy

I wish to define the worshiping community as a *circle of empathy*.[1] I believe that this definition can include small prayer groups, youth groups, even Sunday School classes: any group in which more than one are gathered for worship, in any particular form, is an empathic community (Matt. 18:20). Empathy is a *feeling* that is often discussed in ministerial practice, usually within the contexts of pastoral care, but empathy is commonly cited as a religious emotion.[2] I will argue that through circles of empathy, solipsistic (that is, solitary or separated) individuals *become* communities.

The word, e*mpathy*, as it happens, originates from 20th century Continental philosophy. The two philosophers most commonly associated with the idea of empathy are the phenomenological thinkers Edmund Husserl and Edith Stein. Through a brief tour through these two philosophers' difficult psychological philosophies, we will come to a better sense of what is meant by the term *empathy*.

Before going any further, a brief reflection upon the relevance of the term *empathy* in today's theoretical climate will prove to be helpful. The idea of empathy is an important element in the theoretical nexus of several professions, including nursing; psychoanalytic psychology; and, as mentioned before, pastoral care. The word *empathy* in the English language comes from the psychologist T. Lipps's 1909 *Leitfaden der Psychologie*, where he coined the term *"Einfühlung"*—*empathy*.[3] For Lipps, empathy was an aesthetic term which referred to an individual "digesting" and processing artistic stimuli, resulting in a "feeling of oneness" with the stimulus or stimuli.[4] This *digestive* process for Lipps was the primary mode for the "I" to know other subjects: he called this mode "primordiality" or "empathy."[5]

Psychologist Heinz Kohut much later brought the idea of empathy into fruition in clinical practice for psychoanalysis.[6] Conversely, most literature within psychoanalytic "self-psychology" today does not historically look before Kohut for clarification regarding the idea of empathy. The academic study of nursing, for example, often acknowledges Kohut as *the* primary theorist for the practice of "empathy"; however, among nursing educators today empathy has simply become pseudonymous with "caring" for patients—or perhaps even the *illusion* of "care" for patients.[7]

Between Lipps and Kohut, the idea of empathy was developed by the phenomenological philosophers Edmund Husserl and Edith Stein. For them, empathy is much more than *caring* for another person; empathy is what two or more people can experience *together* to attempt to lessen the distance between a person and another person or persons' experiences.[8] To this end, I will briefly explore the phenomenological foundations of empathy in the thought of Husserl and Stein in order to re-claim the philosophical foundation of *empathy*—which is much more than a construal of *care*—for the purpose of constructing *religious community*.

EDMUND HUSSERL'S
PHENOMENOLOGICAL EMPATHY

According to Edmund Husserl's *Cartesian Meditations*, within an individual's "sphere of ownness" (that is, the *circle* of reality that we *construct* around ourselves) empathy may occur upon another person through an association involving one's own material and affective knowledge of oneself. Since Husserl believes that living and experiencing other*s* is a "given" (a fact that can be assumed about the world), empathy seems at first to occur only between two individuals, the "couple."[9]

For Husserl, any conception of *community* beyond two individuals is, more or less, impossible. In his *Meditations* Husserl defines community simply as coming into contact with another person through empathy. But, if empathy is a process through which one enters into a "co-existence" with an "other," where two individuals experience a "collusion" of realities (what he calls a "*common time-form*"), can such a collusion genuinely occur among more than two individuals? Husserl writes:

> If with my understanding of someone else, I penetrate more deeply into him, into his own horizon of ownness, I shall soon run into the fact that, just as his animate bodily organism lies in my field of perception and that, in general, he experiences me forthwith as an Other for him, just as I experience him as *my* Other. Likewise I shall find that, in the case of a plurality of others, they are experienced also by one another as Others, and consequently that I can experience any given Other not only as himself an Other but also as related in turn to *his* Others and perhaps . . . related at the same time to me.[10]

With the "deep penetration" of empathic knowledge of the other,* then, not only does the other enter into my own sphere of ownness, but a "network" of ownness occurs. As my reality collides with another person's reality, this network of two realities becomes *synchronized*—simply through an acquaintance! At first glance, this network suggests that I simply gain more skills for empathizing with others as my empathic skills grow by "networking" with a multiplicity of persons—such an interpretation is, in my reading, a far cry from entering into a co-existence, common time-form, or *collusion* of realities with the other. For such a collusion of realities to occur simply by association or acquaintance does not seem to me to be an *authentic* or *genuine* practice for entering large groups of individuals into a shared sphere of ownness.

While my interpretation of this quotation from Husserl may be a bit literal,[11] Husserl wrote more upon the idea of community in his posthumously-published *Ideas II*. Since individuals live in an originally-given *zoa* (that is, our assumed reality), Husserl writes that we must naturally assume that "mutual relations" and "communication" between "man and man" and "men and animals" occur. Furthermore, "more simple and more complex social connections" are given, including "friendships, marriages, unions; these are connections instituted between men (on the lowest level, already between animals)."[12] These "simple and complex social connections," however, are only addressed by Husserl as social phenomena in which one may empathize with others, but never explained these connections as a unit or foundation of a community.[13]

Regardless, "community" to Husserl does not seem to be a shared *meta-sphere of ownness* (or an actually *shared* reality), but community is instead a shared "referential" togetherness which has, at its base, empathy. He writes that within the "system of appresentations. . . . the case of the solipsistic subject, has its original basis in original connectors of regular co-existence in such a way that the connected members and senses of members in their *co-presence* are not just there together but refer to one another." "This system," he says, "develops as a system of ordered individuals only by means of continuous experience of other people, who are already constituted by empathy."[14] This referential togetherness does not imply a *collusion* of realities other than a shared commitment to empathy and community. Intersubjectivity arises when there is clarity that "I can be aware of you" and "you can be aware of me," and *we share a commitment to empathize with each other for our shared goals*: experiencing each other's feelings and becoming aware of ourselves through each other (the "thereness-of-me" in the other)—but not necessarily in a group setting "deeply penetrating each other."[15]

Feelings then become the foundation for a community insofar as feelings are what is shared between individuals through empathy in community. Through

---

* By this term, "the other," I am using a psychoanalytic and philosophical term that means an *other person*.

empathy, Husserl writes, "I encounter bodies," that is to say, I encounter "material things of the same type as the material things constituted in solipsistic experience": namely, "my body." Through feeling "by empathy" I know that in another body "there is an Ego-subject" whose sensual feelings may be transferred to me through the deep penetration of empathy. Empathy is both the means and end of deep penetration, as empathy is both the process and the state of knowing the interiority of the other, namely her feelings, through associative referential togetherness with my own. This knowledge is, again, completely hinged upon the material knowledge of the local I—especially upon the knowledge and awareness of the relation between my own feelings and my own bodily experience.[16]

In *Ideas II*, Husserl writes that co-presence must be established before empathy. Once co-presence is established between individuals—once empathy is directly (or indirectly) established as the possible basis of a proposed relationship—then the empathic process may occur. A bodily relationship which requires psychical intimacy must, in addition to self-knowledge of the individuals' own self-experience, have an established co-presence to function empathically.[17] Husserl suggests that through an established co-presence the interiority of psychic acts, the feelings, are finally transferred. He explains:

> What is then understood is psychic being, which is co-given to the spectator along with the Bodily movements in co-presence, and indeed as conforming to rules, movements which now for their part frequently become new signs, that is, for the psychic lived experiences which have indicated or surmised earlier in another fashion. Gradually, in this way, a system of indications is formed, and there is finally in actuality an analogy between this system of signs "expressing" psychic events, both the active and the passive, and the system of signs of language for the expression of thoughts, abstracting from the fact that language itself, as actually spoken, also belongs to the former system.[18]

Through analogy with the other, when in authentic and empathic co-presence, an I enters a relationship with the other, using a language which is only genuinely knowable within their sphere of ownness. As such, a mutual dependence grows between the two in their search for true community and meaning in a Babelic world which does not speak the same language as fully as those within the "sphere."[19]

In sum, this process, while explained somewhat erratically, may be compiled into eight movements. When individuals (1) have self-knowledge of their own bodily experience, (2) they *agree*, directly or indirectly, to enter into a co-presence with each other. In this agreement, the individuals (3) penetrate each other's psychic realms deeply through entering each other's spheres of ownness. As such, (4) a system of indications is formed, which leads (5) the local I to see herself not only as a subject but an objectively-related subject from the point of view of the other. This conception of the self results in a (6) *genuine co-presence*—a referential togetherness—established through this empathic process, where (7) the feelings, or the interiority of the other may be authentically known. Finally, (8) a mutual dependence occurs between individuals as the relationship matures and grows "deeper." This relationship is always spatial: it is a bodily relationship of "being-somewhere" with another: being "here" as opposed to everything else ("there").[20]

But is not retaining one's sense of self always an identification of the other as "there," as opposed to "here"—that is, "you," as opposed to "me"?[21] For Husserl, "I" cannot become "you"; but through empathy, I can see myself as a "you": this is the "thereness-of-me" in the other. In other words, the empathic relationship is based upon a spatial and bodily configuration, but my psychical penetration of the other's interiority is beyond the "thing-itself" which I initially perceive in the object of the other's body.[22] This end-point of accepting subjectivity suggests to me that Husserl has in a way "begged the question" in his investigation of empathy. More specifically, while Husserl does seem to break out of a Cartesian solipsism, his assumption is that since subjectivity is in fact subjective, and "I" subjectively know that I subjectively come into contact with others who appear to behave as subjects themselves, "subjectivity," as Natalie Depraz writes, "is from the very start intersubjectivity."[23] While I am willing to accept intersubjectivity as a given, based upon the givenness of subjectivity, Husserl was correct to be suspicious of his own conclusions, as I do not think his conclusions could survive his own solipsistic scrutiny.[24]

Beyond this objection, I question whether Husserl's understanding of empathy is motivated by an individual wishing to know an other or as a human experience of phenomenologically collecting data.[25] I suggest that Husserl made such an effort to discuss empathy (a topic which could potentially invalidate his system and method) out of an *ethical* concern. In other words, at the end of phenomenology, which is the philosophical "science" of the self's coming into genuine relation with objects, a new way of thinking remains—perhaps *meta-phenomenologically*—for the self to come into a genuine relation with people. Nonetheless, Husserl seemed to want to employ a similar methodology in his treatment of empathy, which appears at times to be little more than the manner by which a local I collects data from the other, if not "using" the other to gain trustworthy knowledge of the self.[26] To be sure, Husserl does not write of what the other gains from an empathic co-presence, other than an assumed intersubjectivity.[27] Critic Forrest Williams writes that "Husserl thinks of the apprehension of others neither as a judgment nor as a merely emotional response, but as a rather complex kind of perception."[28] In this sense, Husserl's conception of empathy might even be thought of as *selfish*, since its ultimate concern appears, by some accounts, as only a manner for collecting data of human objects, which, though similar to animal objects, are different from other objects.

By my account, the end goal for Husserl is to not only learn how to live genuinely with other human beings, but also to understand human feelings—which can only be understood from the subjective experience of empathy with an other.[29] Dan Zahavi writes that ultimately "the self-givenness of the other is inaccessible and transcendent to me... it is exactly this limit" for Husserl that "I can experience." "The otherness of the other," then, " is exactly *manifest* in his elusiveness and inaccessibility." To demand more would be "a negation of the alterity of the other, of that which makes the other other."[30] As such, empathy is not an end in itself, but a mode of being-with-others, and, more importantly to the phenomenologist, is the *utility* by which Husserl seeks to overcome the phenomenological "problem of other minds."

EDITH STEIN
AND *THE PROBLEM OF EMPATHY*

Edith Stein—known to some Catholics as Saint Teresa Benedicta of the Cross—is perhaps best known to the English-speaking world as a controversial saint, a Jewish woman who was taken to her death at Auschwitz as a Franciscan sister. (Stein announced to her family as a teenager that she was an atheist, but while as a young woman studying phenomenological philosophy she converted to Catholicism and later joined a Franciscan convent.)[31] Stein was one of Edmund Husserl's finest students, and her most famous work, *On the Problem of Empathy*, took on Husserl's idea of empathy.

While some critics readily believe that Stein did little more than clarify and validate Husserl's conclusions about empathy, such opinions arise from a "liberal" reading of Husserl and a "conservative" or religiously secular reading of Stein.[32] There is, however, some evidence that Stein and Husserl were very similar in their philosophies regarding empathy. Stein scholar Michael Andrews, for example, has speculated that Husserl indefinitely postponed the publication of *Ideas II* because of the overly-abundant presence of Stein's editing of the text, which occurred while she worked as his assistant.[33] A letter from Husserl to Stein writes that "I have an impression . . . that in your work you forestall some material that is in my second part of *Ideas*."[34] I will show in this chapter how Stein employs Husserl's solipsistic method and, at first glance, seems to only confirm and validate Husserl's methodology on empathy; but a closer reading will show significant additions *to* and deviations *from* Husserl's project that significantly developed the idea of empathy in the early 20th century. After investigating Husserl and Stein, I will turn to their conclusions regarding empathy to attempt to develop an idea of *community*, relying heavily upon both philosophers' understandings of *empathy* and *feeling*.

In *On the Problem of Empathy*, Stein places herself to be in a direct conversation with Husserl on the "problem" of empathy—recognizing that empathy is in fact a significant stumbling block for Husserl's phenomenology.[35] At times her book seems to be having an inside conversation with Husserl; however, other individuals are present in the philosophical background of her narrative, including T. Lipps, William Dilthey, and Max Scheler.[36] Although Stein reiterated the importance of the problem of empathy in phenomenology by employing Husserl's method, she deviated from Husserl by, as Peter Gorday writes, "clarifying" how "empathy can be said to be 'primordial' in Husserl's sense by noting the quality of primordiality" of the self, as Stein wrote, that "the experience that an I has of an I."[37] In other words, for Stein, in the first place, we are *feeling* persons who can self-actualize our feeling for others. We are not machines who simply use feelings to explore the world; instead, through empathy we discover others in the world, and we discover ourselves as selves in the world.

Obviously, the most salient issue in *On the Problem of Empathy* is empathy itself, which she quickly defines "as the perceiving of foreign subjects and their experience." Since this empathic concern is directly involved with human interaction, phenomenology, Stein notes, will be the philosophical method by which her investigation will lead. As a philosophical venture, Stein states that her investigation is justifiably located within the disciplinary realm of philosophy because

> [t]he goal of phenomenology is to clarify and thereby to find the ultimate basis of all knowledge. To reach this goal it considered nothing that is in any way 'doubtful,' nothing that can be eliminated . . . . the entire surrounding world, the physical as well as the psycho-physical, the bodies as well as the souls of men and animals (including the psycho-physical person of the investigator himself) is subject to the exclusion of reduction.[38]

Later in the book, Stein clarifies the nature of philosophy as the discipline of "clarity."

> [T]here is no longer any discipline into which it can push unsolved questions as all disciplines can. This means that philosophy must give the final answer, gain final clarity. We can have final clarity and no questions remain open when we have achieved what we call progress—the constitution of transcendental objects in an immanently given, pure consciousness. This is the goal of philosophy.[39]

In other words, Stein views her investigation at first as a strictly philosophical enterprise—but she concludes with particularly *theological* aspirations. Like Husserl, when approaching objects, Stein believes that we are able to experience the "full phenomenon" of things, including "the foreign psychic life of other subjects." To this end, when observing another person, Stein writes, "I not only know what is expressed in facial expressions and gestures, but also what is hidden behind them."[40] Stein's project is to understand the resulting *feelings* which result from approaching others: how do the "objects" of the "psychophysical" arise?[41]

When an I experiences sadness as a result of another person's grimace, Stein writes, the foreign subject's sadness is not what the original percieving subject experiences. The subject's sadness is not primordial; therefore, the sadness does not claim its immediate "I" as its subject.[42] This *empathy*, however, is not just an *imitation*, since imitation is when a "witnessed gesture arouses in me the impulse to imitate"—to the contrary, this imitation is not empathy because it is on the level of gesture, not an authentic or authenticated *feeling*. Imitation-as-such "does not serve a cognitive function": imitation does not arouse *feeling*."[43]

What makes an action *empathetic*, then, is when first "another's expression [reminds] me of one of my own so that I ascribe to his expression the usual meaning for me."[44] In other words, one person's expression of feeling invokes one of my own memories of feeling myself, for example: "I remember what it feels like to smile." But just more "fully perceiving" the other is not enough for an empathic relation to the other. Following the imitation by analogy, *reflection* of the "inner perception" of the analogy must take place for empathy to be authentic.[45]

Complicating matters for Stein is that when the I experiences another's feelings empathically, it is not the given I which experiences the empathized feelings, but another I which relates the feelings to memories.[46] When a subject perceives the other's face as experiencing pain, a hidden I within the subject remembers a memory which resulted in a similar facial expression, connecting the subject's pain to the other's experience. Simply connecting the experience of the other to my own memories, however, is not enough to be considered empathy—some would say that Husserl ended his understanding here. Instead, as my remembering I "reproduces the structure of [the other's] prior experience," empathy occurs when the structures are not only remembered or connected, but emotionally "digested" and experienced again by myself in a manner which seems to shrink—if not give the *illusion* of shrinkage—the perceptive distance between myself and the other. David Smith calls this shrinkage the *"structural transformation"* of the other's plane of experience. Smith elaborates on Stein:

> I am not actually having the other's experience, and I am not the same person as the other, the enduring subject of her stream of consciousness. Yet in empathy it is *as if* I were feeling her sorrow. Thus, the structure of my experience of empathizing with her sorrow is a certain modification of the structure of her experience.

Again, it is not enough for empathy to be present with a person and to listen and make connections of "referential togetherness" with one's own experiences, and even not enough to experience an emotion with the other, but one must *communicate* that experience to the other, as D. Smith states, so that my experiencing of the other's pain is a *structural transformation*, "projecting myself into the other's place."[47] Again, the circle of perception between two individuals shrinks, and my genuine experience of the other becomes a genuine experience of the other.

But why do we empathize with other humans differently than, for example, cars? Upon this issue, I believe, is where the murkiness of the problem of empathy splits Husserl and Stein. Stein writes that because we understand our bodies to be "zero points" for experiencing, we infer "con-primordially" that others feel and perceive the world similarly to ourselves.[48] This is to say, we recognize the other as an experiencing subject who is not unlike our own local I: Stein calls this "reiterated empathy."[49] Evan Thompson explains:

> In reiterated empathy, I see myself from your perspective . . . . I empathically grasp your empathic experience of me. As a result, I acquire a view of myself not simply as a physical thing but as a physical-thing-empathically-grasped-by-you-as-a-living-being. In other words, I do not merely experience myself as a sentient being from within; nor grasp myself as also a physical thing in the world; I experience myself as recognizably sentient 'from without,' that is, from your perspective, the perspective of another. In this way, one's sense of self-identity, even of the most fundamental levels of embodied agency, is inseparable from recognition by another, and from the ability to grasp that recognition empathetically.[50]

Reiterated empathy, then, is the goal of all empathic activity: by genuinely *attempting* to know and understand (with special emphases on *attempting*) another perceiving I through empathy, the "zero-point" ego can better know herself. The best method by which to know myself, then, is through reciprocated empathizing with another.

In the final section of *On the Problem of Empathy*, Stein makes the interesting and bold claim that "[a]ll outer perception is carried out in spiritual acts." Furthermore, "in every literal act of empathy, i.e., in every comprehension of an act of feeling, we have already penetrated into the realm of the spirit."[51] In other words, Stein makes the analogy that the physical is to perception, as the spiritual is to feeling. Stein adds:

> As my own person is constituted in spiritual acts, so the foreign person is constituted in empathically experienced acts. I experience his every action as proceeding from a will and this, in turn, from a feeling. Simultaneously with this, I am given a level of his person and a range of values in principle experienceable by him.

With the empathic action, one can "glimpse into the kernel of the person"—an action which carries great responsibility.[52]

I interpret Stein's final discourse on the "spiritual plane" of empathy to be saying that to *not* act empathically, to *not* take seriously the true wonder in partaking the human expression of empathy, or to abuse any empathic relationship is a "crime against spirit"; which is to say, *a crime against God*, an irrational or senseless act. Beyond this, when empathy authentically occurs between two persons, the empathy is likely known only to the subjects experiencing the empathy and to God, so that empathy can be known as a kind of miracle or divine gift.[53] Stein believes that the content of human meaning is greatly aided by, if not dependent and sustainable upon, empathy.

Given the religious import of her final conclusions, Stein concludes at the end of *On the Problem of Empathy* that she is well beyond the limitations of philosophy and any kind of "objectivity" offered by the "science" of phenomenology (which she earlier called the discipline of "clarity"). She closes with a sentence containing an unidentified pronoun, which I assume is represented by her term *empathy*: "It is not clear."[54]

CONCLUSIONS

While both Husserl and Stein acknowledge, to varying degrees, that empathy is an extraordinarily slippery area for their phenomenological inquires, in the end there is a subtle difference between their conclusions. For Husserl, empathy is something that just seems to happen: empathy regularly occurs on a daily basis. Stein, on the other hand, believes that often what might appear to alien subjects to be empathy in an experiencing I may really be the I *imitating* the other or *imitating empathy*. For Stein empathy is not necessarily a natural reaction—though she uses examples of children and mothers prevalently in the beginning of her inquiry (the same human object-relation upon which, for example, Heinz Kohut's empathic inquiry is based)—but her understanding of empathy is more of an *achievement* that two perceiving objects must together make an effort to *earn*.[55] Furthermore, I seriously question whether Stein's phenomenological conclusions should be considered, like Husserl's, to be *solipsistic*, since for Stein the emphasis on the other leads to an understanding of the world in which others *must* be encountered, if for no other reason than for the zero-point ego to get to know herself better.

Common to both Husserl and Stein is a problem with the idea of *intimacy*—communal or otherwise.[56] For Husserl, as discussed before, the idea of community may be a problematic concept for his solipsistic system. For Stein, on the other hand, intimacy is implied within the religious experience of empathizing with the other; however, it is not clear for Stein how one can ensure that the feelings transcribed from the other to the local self's memory always find the correct memory and do not lead into fantasy. Beyond this, while I believe that Stein's ultimate goal for practicing empathy is a sustained or sustaining community, what one *does* with the information gathered from the data-collecting empathy of Husserl is never answered. Finally, neither of these thinkers explain *why* we enter into empathy with others.[57]

Most importantly, both thinkers imply that empathy is a salient element—if not *the* salient foundation—of a sustained or sustaining community. I suspect that the reason why empathy is essential to community is because it is, again, implied that *feelings* have something to do with the cohesion of healthy communities. In other words, based upon our inquiry of Husserl and Stein, an empathizing community—which is to say, a community rooted in *feeling*—exists in a shared co-presence where not only the life-world(s) of those in community are recognizable to each other, but a genuine effort has been made on the part of all communal participants to have feeling for one another. The communal members, then, *empathize* with one another on a regular basis.

Communal empathizing which evokes feelings, in my estimation, occurs in its most powerful form in public ritual. The communal nature of funerals, for example, provides families, civic communities, social organizations (as in the case of the Masonic burial ritual), and religious communities the opportunity to empathize together and to have feeling for one another *together*. Most of these rituals are often identified primarily within religious communities: birth, baptism, puberty, marriage, unction, etc. These rituals in religions are typically "open to the public" and identify communal boundaries as *circles of empathy* at any given time.

Edith Stein is correct to connect the idea of empathy to the religious, since true community based upon empathy rarely happens outside of the genuine intimacy offered within occasional pockets of ritualized space and time. For a community to sustain itself as relevant to its members and to those outside of the communal boundaries, *feeling* must occur between the community's individuals in order that empathy might occur. Without empathy, a community is based only upon ideology and not necessarily based in the ultimacy of the human realities of the community's individuals—what is sometimes called the "quasi-religious." Without empathy or without communal feeling, a community is only *imitating* a genuine care and shared foundation in human reality. *Empathy*, then, must be understood as the ground rule for *community*.

Worshiping communities are circles of empathy; they are spaces in which feelings may be shared, ritualized, reciprocated, honored, voiced, and memorialized. In a world that is increasingly isolating and culturally poisonous, genuine circles of empathy are becoming increasingly rare. Next, we will explore not only how our brains are wired in such a way that they actually *hinder us* from empathy and community, but also how our brains are designed to *overcome* our solipsistic ways and enter into circles of empathy.

Notes: Chapter Two

1. I derive this term partially from James F. White's term "liturgical circle," in James White, "Worship and Community," *Doxology* 2 (1985): 23-34.

2. Cf. Gibson, 35-36.

3. T. Lipps, *Leitfaden der Psychologie* (Leipsig: Engelmann, 1909); Arnold Buchheimer, "The Development of Ideas About Empathy," *Journal of Counseling Psychology* 10.1 (1963), 62.

4. Susan Higgins, *The Effect of a Training Program to Improve Abilities in the Accurate Perception of Emotion and Facilitate Skills in Undergraduate Music Therapy Students*, unpublished M.M. thesis (Western Michigan University, 1979), 16.

5. Peter Gorday, *Empathic Knowing and Mystical Knowing*, unpublished M.Th. thesis (Columbia Theological Seminary, 1995), 18.

6. Cf. Heinz Kohut, *The Analysis of the Self* (Madison, CT: International Universities, 1971); *The Chicago Institute Lectures*, ed. Paul Tolpin (Hillsdale, IL: Analytic); and *How Does Analysis Cure?*, ed. Arnold Goldberg and Paul Stpansky (Chicago: U Chicago P, 1984).

7. See, for example, Nancy Eisenberg, "Empathy and Sympathy," *A Handbook of Emotions*, 2nd ed., ed. Michael Lewis and Jeanette Haviland-Jones (New York: Guliford, 2000): 677-691; Gorday, 1-12ff; and Judith Shackelford, *The Nature and Evolution of Phenomenological Empathy in Nursing*, Ph.D. dissertation (The University of Texas at Austin, 1985)—who employs the term phenomenology in a very general sense throughout her work but at no point acknowledges the philosophical origin of the term *empathy*.

8. Cf. S. Toombs, "The Role of Empathy in Clinical Practice," *Journal of Consciousness Studies* 8:5-7 (2001), 249.

9. I find it worth mentioning that this "given" is apparently so strong a given for Husserl, that he seems to transcend his phenomenological method to make such a claim.

10. Edmund Husserl, *Cartesian Meditations* (*CM*), in *The Essential Husserl*, ed. Donn Welton (Bloomington, IN: Indiana UP, 1999), sec. 55-56 (p. 152-157).

11. To be sure, this "literal" interpretation is suggested by Donn Welton, in *The Other Husserl* (Bloomington, IN: Indiana UP, 2000), 153.

12. Edmund Husserl, *Ideas Pertaining to a Pure Phenomenological Philosophy, Second Book* (*Ideas II*), trans. Richard Rojcewicz and André Schuwer (Dordrecht, The Netherlands: Kluwer, 1989) sec. 43 (p. 170). Cf. James Hart, *The Person and the Common Life* (Dordrecht: Kluwer, 1992), 288.

13. Cf. Husserl, *CM*, sec. 51 (p. 210-211).

14. *Ibid*. sec. 45 (p. 173). Some critics of Husserl emphasize the notion of co-presence as more than a "being-with-each-other" or as a safe starting point for the collusion of realities which I ascribe to the goal of entering into a sphere of ownness with an other. Joseph Kockelmans, for example, describes the experience of being inside a sphere of ownness differently, as a process of "mundanizing" (Joseph Kockelmans, *Edmund Husserl's Phenomenology* (West Lafayette, IN: Purdue UP, 1994), 285).

15. Gorday 18; cf. A. Smith, *Routledge Philosophy Guidebook to Husserl and the Cartesian Meditations* (London: Routledge, 2003), 219.

16. Husserl, *Ideas II*, sec. 45 (p. 172, 173-174). Cf. A. Smith, 216.

17. *Ibid.,* sec. 45 (p. 174), sec. 46 (p. 175).

18. *Ibid.,* sec. 45 (p. 174).

19. *Ibid,.* sec. 47 (p.178-179). Evan Thompson, on the other hand, interprets Husserl quite differently, that such linguistic implications cannot be concluded from this idea of empathy; rather, only hypothesizing and inferring can occur (Evan Thompson, "Empathy and Consciousness," *Journal of Consciousness Studies* 8:5-7 [2001], 16). To be sure, the failure of Husserl's theory is that there cannot be certainty about a semiotic relationship between persons rooted in empathy; however, the sphere of ownness does not simply close when all data is collected: instead, as far as I can tell from Husserl, the sphere continues as long as there is a relationship between the two individuals.

20. Husserl, *Ideas II,* sec. 46 (p. 174, 176).

21. Cf. A. Smith 225, 235.

22. Michael Andrews, *Contributions to the Phenomenology of Empathy,* unpublished Ph.D. diss. (Villanova University, 2002). 106; Husserl, *Ideas II,* sec. 47 (p. 177); Frederick Elliston, "Husserl's Phenomenology of Empathy," in *Husserl: Expositions and Appraisals,* ed. Frederick Elliston and Peter McCormick (Notre Dame, IN: U Notre Dame P, 1977), 223.

23. Natalie Depraz, "The Husserlian Theory of Intesubjectivity as Alteriology," *Journal of Consciousness Studies* 8:5-7 (2001), 169; cf. A. Smith, 222.

24. There is, of course, speculation that this is the reason why *Ideas II* was not published during his lifetime.

25. Cf. Forrest Williams, "Intersubjectivity: A Brief Guide," *Husserl's Phenomenology,* ed. J. Mohanty and William McKenna (Washington, DC: Center for Advanced Phenomenology and University Press of America, 1989), 319.

26. Cf. Dan Zahavi, "Beyond Empathy: Phenomenological Approaches to Intersubjectivity," *Journal of Counsciousness Studies* 8:5-7 (2001), 160. Cf. Gorday, 19.

27. Gorday, for example, goes so far to suggest that Husserl is not even concerned with figuring out how intersubjectivity might happen, instead Husserl only *suggests* that empathy might lead to a *possibility* for intersubjectivity (Gorday, 19).

28. F. Williams, 319; cf. Elliston, 227.

29. Zahavi, 159; Andrews, 105.

30. Zahavi, 153; cf. A. Smith, 225.

31. See Edith Stein, *Selected Writings,* trans. Susanne Batzdorff (Springfield, IL: Templegate, 1990), 13ff., 103ff.; *ibid., Essential Writings,* ed. John Sullivan (Maryknoll, NY: Orbis, 2002); Sylvie Courtiny-Denamy, *Three Women in Dark Times,* trans. G. Goshgaran (Ithaca, NY: Cornell UP, 2000); Hilda Graff, *The Scholar and the Cross: The Life and Work of Edith Stein* (London: Longmans, 1955); and Harry Cargas, ed., *The Unnecessary Problem of Edith Stein* (Lanham, MD, UP America, 1994); and Eloise Rosenblatt, "Canonizing Edith Stein and Recognizing Catholic Antisemitism," in *"Good News" after Auschwitz?: Christian Faith Within a Post-Holocaust World,* eds. Carol Rittner and John Roth (Macon, GA: Mercer UP, 2001): 45-68.

32. Dermot Moran and Timothy Mooney, *The Phenomenology Reader* (London: Routledge, 2002), 231.

33. Andrews, 6, 91, 114-132, 412-413.

34. Husserl, quoted from a letter to Stein, in Andrews, 116.

35. Edith Stein, *On the Problem of Empathy,* 3rd rev. ed., trans. W. Stein (Washington, DC: ICS, 1989).

36. Angela Bello, "Edith Stein's Contribution to Phenomenology," *Phenomenology World-Wide*, ed. Anna-Teresa Tymieniecka (Dorderecht, Netherlands: Kluwer, 2002), 232.
37. Gorday, 21; Stein, *Problem of Empathy*, 11.
38. Stein, *Problem of Empathy*, 3.
39. *Ibid.*, 38.
40. *Ibid.*, 5.
41. *Ibid.*, 37.
42. *Ibid.*, 7-11.
43. *Ibid.*, 22, 23; Brian Barnes, *Versions of Empathy* (M.A. thesis, University of Louisville, KY, 1997), 2ff.
44. Stein, *Problem of Empathy*, 27.
45. *Ibid.*, 29-30.
46. *Ibid.*, 39.
47. D. Smith, *The Circle of Acquaintance* (Dordrecht: Kluwer, 1989), 115, 116.
48. Stein, *Problem of Empathy*, 63, 57.
49. *Ibid.*, 63.
50. Thompson, 19-20. Toombs clarifies: "in empathy I have a direct awareness of the other as an embodied individual *like me* (as a *living body* in contrast to a purely physical body). The living body (in contrast with the physical body) is grasped in terms of [the following] important characteristics: I recognize it as animated by its own fields of sensations, as another center of orientation of the spatial world ['zero point'] and...expressive of experience" (249).
51. Stein, *Problem of Empathy*, 92.
52. *Ibid.*, 109.
53. Cf. Gorday, 63.
54. Stein, *Problem of Empathy*, 118.
55. My position on this matter falls somewhat outside of the mainstream of Stein scholarship: for example, Angela Bello writes that Stein's conclusions are exactly the same as Husserl's. Furthermore, he suggests that Stein's importance to the history of phenomenology is precisely that she validated Husserl's methods and claims (Bello, 232).
56. Cf. Barnes, 45-49.
57. Barnes, 18.

Chapter Three
The Neuroscience of Emotion and Feeling

The idea that changes in emotion or feelings have a physiological basis may be as ancient as the first humans' development of rituals.[1] This idea, in my view, assumes a connection between the existential experience of public ritual and the human ontological condition. Today it is not controversial, based upon common human experience, that some connection is present between our affections and our bodies on a physiological level. Obvious examples of this include sweating, breath and heartbeat repetition, skin temperature, and sexual response; obviously, our bodies react to our feelings and outside emotive influences. On a less obvious level, our mental states physiologically affect blood pressure, papillary response, skin reactions, gastrointestinal motility, and chemical balances of bodily fluids.[2]

Among neuroscientists today is a common agreement on this point, namely, that emotions and human physiology are related; and furthermore, they agree that there is a necessary connection between emotion and the physiological structures of the brain. *How* feelings arise from the brain and *which* structures in the brain are responsible for the origins of feeling are, however, disputed.[3] Beyond this, neurological scientists generally agree that there is not a *single* physiological structure in the brain responsible for feelings and emotions, but instead *several areas* of the brain work in concert *together*; how these areas work together is disputed and unknown.[4] Similarly, we may consider a clear relationship between how feelings and emotions develop within the brain and the means by which we learn, create memories, and phenomenologically construct reality around us, but how exactly this happens is similarly unknown and speculative. Despite the uncertainty and controversial nature of this subject area, we will proceed forward in our practical-theological investigation, but with *caution*.[5]

"HEBBIAN SYNAPTIC PLASTICITY"[*]

To be sure: the basic assumptions regarding affective neuroscience, as just mentioned, are that there is a connection between feelings and the brain and that different areas of the brain work together in bringing about such a connection. But if they work together, we may not speak in terms of an *exclusively* "funny" area of the brain, or an *exclusive* "love" area, or an *exclusive* depression area of the brain; but rather, on a micro-cellular level, neural systems change and morph in reaction to external stimuli to bring about emotions.

This theory is called "Hebbian plasticity," named after its original theorist, D. O. Hebb, and refers to the flexibility and malleability—that is, the *plasticity*—of the brain in bringing about emotions. In 1946, Hebb suggested in a *Psychological Review* article that the brain does not simply "switch on" a happy feeling or a sad feeling, but that feelings may suddenly change; feelings do not have to be clearly singular feelings (that is, that happiness and sadness can occur together); and that emotions do not occur as a result of definite combinations of external stimuli, but rather, they are *situational*.[6] A few years later, in 1949, Hebb postulated that human emotions operate in "phase sequences;" in other words, emotions arise as a result of varying combinations of "different neural interactions" within the brain—though *how* and *which* brain components do this was not yet intelligible to him.[7] The term, "plasticity," in relation to neurology, was coined by Jerzy Konorski in 1968, who defined plasticity as the situation when "certain permanent functional *transformations* arise in particular systems of neurons as the result of appropriate stimuli or their combinations."[8] Later experiments and theories by Jerzy, T. Bliss, T. Lømo, Eric Kandel, James Schwartz, Carla Shatz, Michael Stryker, Jeansok Kim, and Mark Baxter (among others) have furthered the theory of Hebbian plasticity, making it a generally accepted and assumed theory among neuroscientists.[9]

Hebb's theory, on the whole, suggests that memory, learning, behaviors, and our *habituative* selves may *arise out of*, and are even *reciprocated* within, the physiological networks and patterns in the brain.[10] The theory does not suggest, however, that memory, learning, behaviors, and habits *originate* in the brain. In other words, our repeated reactions to external stimuli, especially when the brain is in development stages, effect the way in which the brain creates neural, synaptic patterns ("neuro-modulatory cholinergic projections").[11] Eric Kandel and Christopher Pittenger further state that Hebb's

---

[*] To keep the discussion of this chapter on point, I have relegated much of the more technical and sophisticated discourse—mostly directly quoting the scientific sources—to the notes.

framework divides the study of memory into two components: the systems problem and the molecular problem. The systems problems of memory is concerned with where in the brain memory is stored and how neural circuits work together to create, process and recall memories. The molecular problem of memory is concerned with the reactions whereby synapses[*] change and information is stored.[12]

Jeansok Kim and Mark Baxter explain:

> On a biological level, a memory system is usually defined as a neural structure (or network of structures) and its interconnections, which together operate on a particular type of information and then participate in the storage of that information, either within the structure itself or elsewhere.[13]

Regardless of *how* memory actually happens, at bottom is the belief that brain systems develop and are shaped by our external experiences, "which means that the synapses involved are changed by experience."[14]

Regarding the *how* of the plasticity theory, while not particularly important for our agenda here, we are given clues to consider toward our question of what happens when our brains accompany us to worship. The primary theory is that within the brain are neurons, nerve cells which transmit electrical impulses; and upon those neurons are synapses, which could be described as connecting antennae that link neural cells' electrical charges.[15] Over time, patterns develop in the firing of synaptic charges, and the dendrites (the "branches on a cell body responsible for the reception of information from the terminal buttons of other neurons") position themselves in *habituated* ways based upon the *range* of repeated branching.[16] As its name indicates, the "plasticity" of this theory is that neural synapses do not always "fire" the same way all of the time, but over time the synapses organize themselves into patterns and their ranges become somewhat limited.[17] Carla Shatz would later characterize this aspect of Hebb's theory by punning, "cells that fire together, wire together."[18] By "firing," the malleable, habitual neural pathways are forged and created, blazed, changed, saved, covered up, or forgotten.[19]

On a neural level, the brain is always changing. There are many ways in which changes can happen for adults after the impressive growth and development that occurs during one's younger years.[20] Patricia Churchland explains:

> There are many possible ways neurons can change. For example, new dendrites might sprout. . . . There might be some extension of existing branches. Existing

---

[*] Eric Kandel defines *synapse* as "[t]he part of contact between two neurons" that is "fired by the presynaptic terminal of one cell (the *presynaptic* cell) and the receptive (dendritic) surface of the other cell (the *postsynaptic cell*)" (*Cellular Basis of Behavior* [San Francisco: Freeman, 1976], 97).

receptors could modify their structure (e.g., a change in subunits of the protein that constitutes the receptor.) Or new receptor sites might be created. In the curtailing direction, pruning could decrease the dendrites or bits of dendrite, and therewith decrease the number of synaptic connections between neurons. Or synapses on remaining branches could be shut down altogether. Additionally, there might be modulation of sodium channels to change the spiking profile of an axon as a function of neuron-neuron interactions. These we call *postsynaptic* changes in the dendrites.

There may also be *presynaptic* changes to the axons. For example, there may be changes in the membrane (changes might emerge or be altered), or new axonal branches may be formed or pruned. Repeated high rates of firing will deplete the neurotransmitter vesicles available for release, and that transient depletion constitutes a kind of memory on the order of 2-3 seconds. One important presynaptic change involves increasing or decreasing the probability that a vesicle of neurotransmitter will be released when a spike reaches the axonal termination of a neuron. . . . Reliability can be modified on a time-scale of a few hundred milliseconds. . . . The synaptic strength can be increased tenfold in less than a second, without having to build new structures.

Even without new dendrites growing or depleting, the brain is capable of making split-second decisions. Churchland continues:

Other presynaptic changes include changing the number of vesicles released per spike or the number of transmitter molecules contained in each vesicle. Finally, the whole neuron might die, taking with it all the synapses it formerly supported, or in certain special regions, a whole new neuron might be born.[21]

"Every one of these changes does occur," she concludes, "though precisely how the various changes casually connect to input signals is still under study, and how these changes across populations of neurons are *orchestrated* remains baffling."[22] According to the theory of Hebbian synaptic plasticity, *this* is how our nervous systems learn about the world, create memories about objects and experiences in the world, and react to the world.[23]

THE DEVELOPMENT OF PLASTICITY

Neural plasticity occurs throughout the human life cycle.[24] When speaking in terms of post-natal development, one might consider two types of plasticity: developmental and post-developmental. Developmental plasticity is plasticity that occurs during infancy, childhood, and the teenage years, and somewhat into young adulthood; post-developmental plasticity occurs during the adult years. In this post-developmental or adult period, plasticity does occur, but synapses are not as malleable as, for example, those of an infant.[25] William Benzon explains that "[v]ery early in life the neurons in the cerebral cortex develop a large number of dendrites," but "as the nervous system continues to mature, always interacting with the world, synapses that are not reinforced *die off*, and perhaps even dendrites and neurons as well." The habits and "dependencies that become wired into the nervous system reflect patterns of dependencies between states in the external world;" and the synapses that remain continue to function and aid in learning and in the creation of memory, within the patterns and *limitations* provided by previous plastic changes.[26]

It is important, however, to recognize that the death or destruction of synaptic pathways is *not* negative; in fact, this is one of the ways that our brains learn. This kind of learning development is inevitable, but *bad* habits or behaviors can be learned or habituated on the neural level—as well as *good* habits and behaviors. Consequently, from an evolutionary perspective the development of learning and memory is not what these neural functions are meant to perform.[27] According to Joseph LeDoux, the brain evolved in such a way "instead to accomplish certain tasks (like detecting danger, finding food and mates, hearing sounds, or moving a limb)."[28] David Buller further explains that

> the brain's plasticity. . . *is* an adaption. Similarly, the immune system's antibody-assembly process is an adaption. Both of these systems are present in current humans because of past selection for their abilities to produce adaptive responses to the demands of the local environment. But here is the crucial point: In both cases, we need to distinguish the processes from its products. The processes (antibody assembly and brain plasticity) are biological adaptions, but not their products (antibodies and functionally specialized brain circuits). . . . The products of these processes are, instead, singly the adaptive response of adaptations to the local environment.[29]

We should be careful to not speak of plasticity in negative terminology, because it is part of our evolutionary or physiological design, and on a much deeper level than simple learning or memory, it helps us adapt for survival. But it can, as it happens, have negative effects.

Some scientists have suggested that oxytocin (or "oxytoxin") is what triggers plastic changes in the brain. Oxytocin is a "neuro-peptide" known to stimulate electrical activity in the brain, and oxytocin is known to "play a key role in social attachment and affiliation in non-human animals."[30] To this end, it has also been discovered to be released in the brain when an animal gives birth.[31] Oxytocin is believed to "loosen" the neural synaptic pathways in an effort toward creating new pathways.[32] It does *not*, however, force us into a strict habituation; rather, oxytocin "specifically affects an individual's willingness to accept social risks arising through interpersonal interactions."[33] Oxytocin is present when we habituate into our patterns and rhythms, to the point that our "well-established" actions become ritualized; and it helps us cope when our ritualized behaviors become interrupted. It does not "instill knowledge," but rather, oxytocin "opens an opportunity for learning new knowledge."[34] We will return to oxytocin later, in the next chapter.

LEARNING, MODULATION, AND MEMORY

Although neural plasticity occurs throughout the human life cycle, at the various stages on the life cycle, plasticity occurs with varying degrees of sophistication.[35] The difference between learning something as an infant and learning something as an adult is largely the complexity with which *associations* and *references* are made *to what we already know*, as well as how drastically the new knowledge modulates the whole of our brain systems. Antonio Demasio writes that "[t]he neural patterns and the corresponding neural images of the objects and events outside [of] the brain are creations of the brain related to the reality that prompts their creation rather than passive mirror images reflecting that reality."[36] In other words, as we look again at an object which we know, we do not see a "replica" of what we knew, but instead, according to Demasio, "[t]he image we see is based on changes that occurred in *our* organisms, in the body and in the brain, as the physical structure of that particular object interacts with the body."[37]

Our bodies sense a familiar object *differently* in *this* moment than before, precisely because we are capable of noticing something *different* that we were preoccupied with before in noticing, or because we are now able to make *new* and *different interactions* with other, previous knowledge.[38] In any given moment, according to Demasio, "the building of... neural patterns is based on the momentary selection of neurons and circuits engaged by the interaction" and "[t]he neural pattern attributed to a certain object is constructed according to the menu of correspondences by selecting and assembling the appropriate tokens."[39] When we encounter something new, our brains have to work to experience it, or when we encounter something new about a familiar object, our brains are forging new neural connections that have not yet been habituated.[40] Giulio Tononi and Gerald Edelman write:

> After habituation sets in (a time when humans report that stimuli tend to fade from consciousness) the same stimuli evoke neural activity exclusively along their specific sensory pathways. These observations suggest that when tasks are automatic and require little or no conscious control, the spread of signals that influence the performance of a task involves a more restricted and dedicated set of circuits that have become "functionally insulated." This produces a gain in speed and precision, but a loss in context-sensitivity, accessibility, and flexibility.

Further:

A change in the degree to which neural activity is distributed within the brain may accompany the transition between conscious, controlled performance and unconscious, automated performance. When tasks are novel, brain activation related to the task is widely distributed; when the task has become automatic, activation is more localized and may shift to a different set of areas.[41]

In other words, when our ritualistic patterns and habits are interrupted, more of our brain needs to function along with the experience—to *adapt*.[42]

Learning—that is, the *adaptation* of our brain to new experiences—and *memory* are not, then, independent functions of the brain which can be pinned down to a single area of the brain, but rather, they occur *throughout* the brain, involving the strengthening, shifting, and modulation of neural synapses.[43] The strength of synaptic connections and the modulatory exchanges (between synaptic connections and different parts of the brain) is called "long-term potentiation," or "LTP." LTP *creates* our memories; the repeating and repetition of functions make the connections—our *memories*—stronger.[44] While there is not a "file cabinet" or "hard drive" in the human brain, there are conditioned and seasoned neural circuits that make our associations and connections incur memory and learned behavior.[45] Walter Freeman further suggests that the fallibility of human memory is thus accounted by the perpetually-changing brain; that is, "what we remember is continually being changed by new learning, when the connections between nerve cells in brains are modified."[46]

The fact that all of us experience the world very differently, even those with very similar upbringings, educations, races, genders, etc., is also a consequence of the connection between learning, memory, and neural plasticity. On a biological level, our brains are very similar, but our "wiring" and "circuitry" have all developed individually.[47] To be sure, it is probably less accurate to say that "all of us experience the world very differently" than to say that *we construct reality based upon how our brains interpret it*. And further: our constructions of reality are, in essence, *who we are*. At bottom, Joseph LeDoux observes, "we are our synapses."[48]

THEORIES OF FEELING

There are several theories on how feelings or emotions emerge out of neural plasticity; we will only discuss a few here. The essence of these theories is that feelings are consequences of plastic, neural reactions to external stimuli.[49] Similar to other experiences, we *habituate* ourselves *within* emotional or feeling states—again, both positively and negatively—based upon the repetition by which we experience the emotions or feelings. As just mentioned, emotions are usually a reaction to external stimuli, but they may also be *intentionally* entered, though they are more easily evoked purposefully if some memories or neural association have been *potentiated* for those particular emotions or their forms.[50]

Brain scientists Eugene d'Aquili, Andrew Newberg, and Vince Rouse have proposed a theory that I call the "operator theory," which proposes two "operator" functions within the human brain: the *existential* operator and the *emotional value* operator. The existential operator, they suggest, "is the function of the mind that assigns a sense of existence or reality to the sensory information processed by the brain." To put it another way, "this operator gives us the sense that what the brain shows us is real." They further explain:

> The presence of an existential operator is implied by the results of several recent studies. In one such study, babies watched a ball roll. . . across a tabletop, and then disappear behind a screen. When the screen was lifted, the babies saw the ball resting against a wall to their right. The experiment was then repeated, and when the screen was lifted, the babies saw the ball resting against the left side of a solid box. The ball was then rolled a third time, but this time, when the screen was lifted, the babies saw the ball resting on the right side of the box. Observation showed that the babies spent a significant longer time staring at the ball that appeared to have rolled through the box.
>
> This was interpreted as a sign that the babies somehow understood the impossibility of what they were seeing—that one solid, real thing can't pass through another—which in turn implies that even babies naturally comprehend the concreteness of reality.

The existential operator, then, is the interpretive function that coordinates the brain's basic assumptions about the world around itself and what its senses are reporting back to the brain.[51]

The emotional value operator is the *interpretive* function that "exists to assign an emotional valence to all the elements of perception and cognition." It is the *hermeneutic lens* through which the brain ascribes emotions to the experiences which the existential operator initially interprets. If we did not have the emotional value operator, d'Aquili, Newberg, and Rouse argue, we would "move through the world like very intelligent robots." This emotional value operator is part of what makes us human; it is, consequently, according to this theory, part of the evolutionary process that contributes to the success of the human species.[52] It makes us place value judgment upon our own survival.

These two operating functions, according to d'Aquili, Newberg, and Rouse, do not work separately, but they instead work together in their interpretive functions. Our current emotional state can taint or guide the existential operator's function, just as the existential operator's function can change our current emotional state to something different, or even new. Because we operate with both existential and emotional functions, the authors suggest that emotions are an essential element of "human reasoning and rational thinking." Since we can only experience the world with a brain and a posited self that *feels*, "the brain ensures that we will pursue survival intensely and passionately."[53]

Now moving to a different theory, affective neuroscientist Jaak Panksepp believes that feelings arise when, as he writes, "*endogenous sensory and emotional systems* within the brain that receive direct inputs from the outside world as well as the neurodynamics of the SELF begin to reverberate with each other's changing neural firing rhythms." This is to say, numerous synaptic firing systems combine in *concert* with one another, and they centrally involve what Panksepp calls the "SELF." The SELF—a "Simple Ego-type Life Form" that exists "deep within the brain"—is a metaphor for the *I-ness* that holds certain synaptic firing patterns and rhythms together as *one* person's brain-system. The SELF is, on one hand, the overall control panel that creates a unified person (or *self*) within a brain; it is what makes *me* uniquely *me*, as the person whose brain is lodged in this particular body. According to Panksepp, the SELF "comes to be represented in widely distributed ways through higher regions of the brain as a function of neural and psychological maturation." [54] It is always there, but it develops, naturally, along with the plastic changes that occur in the brain throughout human development.

The SELF is not only a human phenomenon, although it is evolved in its most sophisticated form, and is common in the brains of other mammalian species. In this sense, we may speak of sharing empathy or identifying with moods of animals, as they also have a coherent SELF that develops along with their animal brains' plasticity.[55] The brains of mammals, after all, are *phylogenetically* related to our brains: in other words, we are connected to animals by virtue of having some similar evolutionary developments.

Panksepp draws a difference between emotions or emotional states—which are the consequence of synaptic firing patterns—and feelings, which express the brain system through the body as a unified whole.[56] Panksepp explains that "[c]onsidering this possibility, I would argue that basic affective states, which initially arise from the changing neurodynamics of a self-representation mechanism, may provide an essential psychic scaffolding for all other forms of consciousness." In other words, he writes, Descartes' famous dictum, *cogito, ergo sum* ("I think, therefore I am"), "might be superceded by a more primitive affirmation that is part of the genetic makeup of animals," namely, "I *feel*, therefore I am."[57]

To reiterate, for Panksepp, the "SELF" is simply the "neural entity" that is the whole of the plastic, neural system out of which affections arise.[58] He explains in more detail of how feelings arise from the brain:

> If affective mood states are ultimately constituted of distinct reverberating neural patterns within the extended SELF-representation networks of the brain, it is possible that each type of mood can be set in motion by a variety of inputs into the system. When the primitive emotional command circuits arouse the whole extended neural network, we have full-blown emotional states. On the

other hand, when cognitive inputs . . . initiate weaker types of reverberation in the system, we have mood states. Thus, because of our past experiences and history of conditioning, cognitions can come to revoke strong feelings.

However, once a weaker type of reverberation has been established, it can proceed along several paths. It has the potential to become a full-blown emotion if the reverberation recruits full arousal of the primitive emotional command systems. . . . However, the reverberation also has the potential to fire rapidly, if one can divert cognitive resources to other points of view.

"This," Panksepp continues, "I believe, is the main aim of various forms of self-discipline, including assisted ones such as cognitive behavior therapy." [59] Therapy, medications, and perhaps rituals can *shake up* our neural connections—that is, they *induce* adult plasticity. He further explains:

Thus, in adult humans, cognitive processes have the option of becoming *enmeshed*, even further, within ongoing emotional dynamics, or they can *extract themselves* from an ongoing neural maelstrom. Emotional self-regulation is presumably made possible through our higher cerebral endowments. Our symbol systems are especially effective in allowing us to negotiate such rough terrain. Language allows us to regulate our emotions.[60]

At bottom, for Panksepp, the theory of the "SELF" offers an opportunity to consider the brain through the variety of factors that intermingle sensual experience, cognition, memory, learning, emotion, and feeling as a unified whole, while acknowledging that we can take some control over our own emotions. That is, we can experience ourselves as "active agents in the perceived events of the world."[61] Through our "SELVES" we are able to become more aware of the world, and as a result, also aware of "our*selves*," and reciprocally so. This ability to influence or own emotional state is the conduit by which we may *liberate* ourselves from our habits, grow, and self-actualize.

Although Panksepp's argument is rooted in science and appears to be more natural philosophy than science (that is, he makes philosophical conclusions based upon scientific hypotheses), his argument is compelling because the argument accounts for a *unity* between the multiplicity of neural networks that connect our sense organs to our brains and our emotions to our feelings. He himself admits that his theory is a "best guess" and speculates that, like nearly all things involving the science and philosophy of the brain, "many centuries of work will be needed to reveal how emotional systems really operate."[62] That being said, we may now consider a philosophical theory of emotion which takes seriously the neuroscience we have available to us in the present situation.

THE "PEAK EXPERIENCE"

Numerous theorists of the science of feelings and emotion write of the "peak experience," that is, an experience that results in "chills," a "skin orgasm," "evanescence," "optimal experience," or "flow."[63] "Peaking" is often associated with enjoyable experiences—especially those arising from visual or musical experiences—as well as religious or "mystical" experience.[64] Peaking is also associated with self-actualization because, as theorist Mihaly Csikszentmihalyi writes, it is *autotelic*: in other words, "it refers to a self-contained activity, one that is done not with the expectation of some future benefit, but simply because the doing itself is the reward."[65]

The phenomena of the autotelic peak experience usually involves "full concentration on the relevant stimuli, total absorption in the activity, altered perception of time, and loss of self-consciousness," as well as "a special flow of wonder, of awe, of reverence, of humility and surrender" or even as "a reluctance to come down from the experience."[66] Alf Gabrielson classifies the kinds of experiences that are reported with peaking into four groups:

1. feelings of loss of something (e.g. loss of time, place, sense, self);
2. feelings of gain of something (e.g. gain of timelessness, release, satisfaction, perfection, new knowledge);
3. feelings of ineffability (e.g. the experience is indescribably, eludes verbal communication); and
4. quasi-physical feelings (e.g. light, heat, improvement, calm, or peace).[67]

Beyond these, peaking will often lead to a profound identification with others, or, as Abraham Maslow explains, with the "whole of the world... as a unity, as a single rich live entity."[68] Self-actualization (*actio immanens*) is, then, connected to a "loss of self."[69]

Robert Panzarella's research of the peak experience reports that only about one in 3,000 people report having experienced peaking, but for those who have experienced peak experiences, peaking is not an entirely rare experience.[70] In addition to visual experiences, nostalgic experiences, athletic experiences, intellectual experiences and games, experiences of nature and solitude, and the experiences of—as well as the making of—music are commonly described as activities out of which peak experiences arise.[71] Panzarella writes that among those who have experienced peaking, 35% report having "peaked" as a response to a musical experience, and 19% as a result of a visual experience; 25% report peaking as a response to music and visual experience together. Peaking can lead, he writes, to a "renewal ecstasy," which results in a perspective that the "world is better," or even a "fusion-emotional ecstasy," where one gains a sense of unity with a deity or common humanity.[72]

Music is a common source that is reported for peak experiences—which is probably a result of the prevalence of music in common religious, social, civic, educational, and leisure activities. Panksepp's research suggests that we attach stronger feelings to songs which we know, and that sad or somber music has a higher response rate for peaking than happy music. Interestingly, according to Panksepp's research, "unfamiliar sad music" had a higher "peak factor" than "familiar happy music."[73] Panksepp also found that peaking with music was much more common for women than with men.[74] I will return to music later.

Peaking may be considered an experience that begins on the physiological level; researchers who have explored the idea of the peak experience, such as Pankseep, work under the assumption that there is an "underlying neurochemical" basis to the experience.[75] The reporting of shivers, rise of heartbeat, uncontrollable physical response (such as a "trance" state) with peaking suggests that peaking is not just a mood or emotion, but rather it the result of certain neural combinations within the whole of the brain.[76] Obviously, peaking is connected to strong emotional arousal and physical response, but more specifically, it is a result of the *plastic* changes that occur within the brain on a neural level.[77] Considering the brain as a unified whole, peaking may be attributed to repetition or physical rhythm: repeated phrases, actions, movements, or thinking patterns that "attempt to recycle the same subroutine over and over again in the nervous system."[78] Panksepp calls these repeated neural codes that lead to peaking "triggers."[79] Much of our daily routines (as discussed earlier) are indeed ritualized and repeated, but few of these repeated activities or patterns are *autotelic*—that is, genuinely done for their own sakes. Mihaly Csikszentmihalyi explains that autotelic peak experiences are

> very different from the feelings we typically have in the course of life. So much of what we ordinarily do has no value in itself, and we do it only because we have to do it, or because were expect some future benefit from it. . . .
>
> The autotelic experience, or flow, lifts the course of life to a different level. Alienation gives way to involvement, enjoyment replaces boredom, helplessness turns into a feeling of control, and psychic energy works to reinforce the sense of the self, instead of being lost in the service of external goals. When experience is intrinsically rewarding, life is justified in the present, instead of being held hostage to a hypothetical future gain.

The peak experience, it seems for Csikszentmihalyi, might be attainable for more than the very few, and is a self-actualizing, potentially *liberative* experience. Like other strong neural functions, peaking is not always necessarily positive, Csikszentmihalyi notes, since "one must be aware of the potentially addictive power of flow."[80]

Conclusion

Returning to the connection between peak experience and music, I can write from my own experience that one of the most distinct peak experiences that I have felt—and in fact, felt with a group—was related to music. Specifically, I am reminded of what would be my final experience, as a senior in high school, in performing with a marching band at the Pennsylvania state marching band championships (which, to be sure, is a surprisingly athletic and physical activity that additionally involves numerous spatial and temporal brain functions at once). There I can recall playing the last notes of our field routine, a version of Nikolai Rimsky-Korsakov's "Russian Easter Overture," and immediately after the last note and exhaling while thundering down my trumpet into a rest position from my sore embouchure, as an immediate response to the drum major's command to do so, I felt a sense of euphoria, chills, and tingly shivers for several moments. While marching off the field to the repetitive cadence of the band's drum-line, I remember other teenage musicians in the band saying to each other, as soon as we were out of the audience's view, that they had experienced something similar.

Today, I experience a remnant of that strong peaking whenever I listen to a recording that I have of that year's state marching band championship competition, or even to a different recording or performance of *Russian Easter Overture*. Beyond this, I also experience peaking "triggering" when listening to other music that has a formal or technical similarity to "Russian Easter Overture," such as the distinctly orchestral counterpoint in V. S. Kalinnikov's *Symphony No. 1* in G Minor (which, consequently, I have also previously performed in a concert band setting). While there is certainly a nostalgia factor at work in my peak experience, I believe that my previous peak experience was so strong that the neural firing patterns that plastically respond to these pieces of music have been emblazed such that the peak experience arises as a kind of memory, thereby creating meaning.[81] The experience opens up for a heightened possibility of triggering a peak experience because of a synaptic memory associated with peaking and the specific experience. Consequently, whenever I have since experienced peaking in other activities—prayer or meditation, singing, viewing films—I am always reminded of my experience marching off of a football field, in step with one hundred other musicians, in Hershey, Pennsylvania.

Over the course of this chapter, I have presented the scientific belief that the brain changes over time and that changes made in the brain are connected to learning, memory, and emotion. Furthermore, there is evidence that a "peak experience" may also have a physiological basis that arises from the synaptic configurations of our brains. Next, I will explore how this kind of neurological paradigm for thinking about the human condition will be helpful in thinking about the act of public worship in religious communities.[82]

Notes: Chapter Three

1. Cf. d'Aquili and Newberg (1999), 106-107.
2. Robert Plutchik, *The Psychology and Biology of Emotion* (New York: HarperCollins, 1994), 137.
3. Hogue, 62.
4. Giulio Tononi and Gerald Edelman, "Consciousness and Complexity," in *Essential Sources in the Scientific Study of Consciousness*, eds. Bernard Baurs, William Bowls, and James Newman (Cambridge, MA: MIT UP, 2003), 995.
5. Panksepp (1998), 304; cf. Hogue, 56; Raymond Dolan and John Morris, "The Functional Anatomy of Innate and Acquired Fear: Perspectives from Neuro-imaging," *Cognitive Neuroscience of Emotion*, eds. Richard Lane and Lynn Nadel (New York: Oxford UP, 2000), 232; and Carla Shatz, "Dividing Up the Neocortex," *Science* 258.5080 (9. October 1992), 237(2).
6. D. Hebb, "Emotion in Man and Animal: An Analysis of the Intuitive Processes of Recognition," *Psychological Review* (1942): 88-106, esp. 104-106. According to Churchland, Hebb's research was based upon—and a rejection of—experiments on rats from the 1920's by Karl Lashley (Churchland, 328ff).
7. D. Hebb, *The Organization of Behavior* (New York: Wiley, 1949), 79; the primary discussion of this theory occurs on pp. 79-106ff.
8. Jerzy Konorski, *Conditional Reflexes and Neuron Organization*, trans. Stephen Garry (New York: Hafner, 1968), 79-80. Cf. Joseph LeDoux, *Synaptic Self: How Our Brains Become Who We Are* (New York: Penguin, 2002), 137.
9. Konorski, 78-92ff.; T. Bliss and T. Lømo, "Long-Lasting Potentiation of Synaptic Transmission in the Dentate Area of the Anaesthetized Rabbit Following the Stimulation of the Perforant Path," *Journal of Physiology*, 232 (1973): 331-336; Eric Kandel and James Schwartz, "Molecular Biology of Learning: Modulation of Transmitter Release," *Science* 218 (29. October 1982): 433-443; Carla Shatz, "Emergence of Order in Visual System Development," *Proceedings of the National Academy of Sciences USA* 93 (January 1996): 602-608; Michael Stryker, "Activity-Dependent Reorganization of Afferents of the Visual System," in *Proceedings of the Retna Research Foundation Symposia*, vol. 3, eds. Dominic Man-Kit Lam and Carla Shatz (Cambridge, MA: MIT UP, 1991): 267-287; and Jeansok Kim and Mark Baxter, "Multiple Brain-Memory Systems: The Whole Does not Equal the Sum of Its Parts," *Trends in Neuroscience* 24.6 (June 2001): 324-330, esp. 327-329.
10. Charles Nelson, Michelle de Haan, and Kathleen Thomas write that "[i]t is important to understand the experiences don't just happen to the brain; rather, experience is the product of an ongoing, *reciprocal interaction* between the environment and the brain" (in *Neuroscience of Cognitive Development: The Role of Experience and the Developing Brain* [Hoboken, NJ: Wiley, 2006], 30, emph. add.).
11. James Pirch, Kathy Turco, and Hubert Rucker, "A Role for Acetylcholine in Conditioning-Related Responses of Rat Frontal Cortex Neurons: Microiontophoretic Evidence" *Brain Research* 586 (1992), 24.
12. Eric Kandel and Christopher Pittenger, "The Past, the Future, and the Biology of Memory Storage," *Philosophical Transactions of the Royal Society of London B* 354 (1999), 2027.

13. Kim and Baxter, 324.
14. LeDoux, (2002), 9.
15. *Ibid.,* 80.
16. Hogue 199, LeDoux (2002), 81.
17. LeDoux (2002), 79. LeDoux elsewhere expounds: "Bliss and Lømo showed that the size of the field potential, and thus the magnitude of the synaptic response, could be increased by a simple manipulation. They zapped the pathway with a brief period of stimulation at a very high rate (one hundred stimulus pulses in a second). The size of the synaptic response elicited by a single pulse test stimulus was bigger after than before the intervening zap. The zap, in other words, increased the strength of the synaptic connection between the transition region and the hippocampus. And most importantly, the changes that were produced appeared to be enduring rather than fleeting. The production of changes in synaptic strength as a result of brief stimulations is usually referred to as 'long-term potentiation' (LTP)" (Joseph DeDoux, *The Emotional Brain* [New York: Touchtone, 1996], 214, 216). Cf. d'Aquili and Newberg (1999), 57.
18. Shatz, in LeDoux (2002), 79.
19. The "paths" or "pathways" referred to here are the "thalamo-amygdala pathways" and the "thalamo-cortio-amygdala pathway." The first, the thalamo-amygdala pathway, which is a "conditioned emotional path" where data is processed "through the thalamus to the amygdala where it is ascribed a positive or negative volence." The second kind, thalamo-cortio-amygdala pathways, involves data going from the thalamus to the cortex and "utilizing cognition" (Allison Feit, *Implicit Affect: Affective Neuroscience, Cognitive Psychology, and Psychopathology and the Emergence of a New Discipline,* unpublished Ph.D. dissertation, Adelphi University [Garden City, NY: 2005], 10). Cf. John Aggleton and Andrew Young, "The Enigma of the Amydgala: On Its Contribution to Human Emotion," *Cognitive Neuroscience of Emotion,* eds. Richard Lane and Lynn Nadel (New York: Oxford UP, 2000), 107-109, 112-114ff; and Hogue, 64. For the purposes of my project, I am generally referring to either kinds of pathways when speaking of neural paths or connections.
20. Cf. Valerie Reyna and Frank Farley, "Is the Teen Brain Too Rational?" *Scientific American Mind* 17.6 (Dec. 2000), 60.
21. Churchland, 330. Further: "[a]ll of the above-mentioned 'modifications'. . . ultimately involve synaptic change, either directly or indirectly, or can be reasonably so construed."
22. *Ibid.* Churchland notes that not all plasticity is technically *Hebbian* plasticity. Hebbian plasticity is (1) "specific to the synapse where the pre- and post-synaptic activity occurs, and (2) it depends *conjointly* on both pre- and post-synaptic cells, but not on the activity of other (connected) cells." If the *plastic* change occurs to the "whole cell" then "the plasticity is non-Hebbian." To be sure, most plasticity that is "postnatal" or includes "classic examples of *learning*" is Hebbian (334). Cf. Nelson, de Haan, and Thomas, 40-43.
23. William Benzon, *Beethoven's Anvil: Music in Mind and Culture* (New York: Basic, 2001), 55.
24. Nelson, Haan, and Thomas, 39; cf. Reyna and Farley, 60.
25. Nelson, Haan, and Thomas, 33; cf. Margaret Mahler, Fred Pine, and Anni Bergman, *The Psychological Birth of the Human Infant* (New York: Basic, 1975), 48-51.
26. Benzon, 55, emph. add.

27. LeDoux (2002), 8; cf. Antonio Damasio, *Looking for Spinoza: Joy, Sorrow, and the Feeling Brain* (Orlando, FL: Harcourt, 2003), 200. Raymond Dolan and John Morris explain differently: "Classical conditioning is a simple form of associative learning in which a neural stimulus acquires behavioral significance (and therefore salience) through its temporal paring with an innately salient unconditioned stimulus. This type of conditioning is manifest across the phylogenetic scale from gastropod mallosis to humans. The associate plastic synaptic changes represent one of the simplest forms of value-dependent neural plasticity. In mammals, this plasticity of neural response appears to depend on neuro-modulatory cholinegeric projections, predominately from the neucleus basalis of Meynert" (Dolan and Morris, 232).

28. LeDoux (2002), 8-9.

29. David Buller, *Adapting Minds: Evolutionary Psychology and the Persistent Quest for Human Nature* (Cambridge, MA: MIT UP, 2005), 141.

30. Michael Kosfeld, Markus Henrichs, Paul Zak, Urs Fischbacher, and Ernst Fehr, "Oxytocin Increases Trust in Humans," *Nature* 435 (2. June 2005), 673; and Yvonne Brackbill, "Obstetrical Medication and Infant Behavior," *Handbook of Infant Development*, ed. Joy Osofsky (New York: Wiley, 1979), 81.

31. Freeman (1997), 70.

32. Benzon, 81. This theory, of course, is only a theory, and is not without its debates and opponents. Jaak Panksepp writes that although "[m]any molecular underpinnings for neuronal plasticity have already been revealed. . . no growth factor or gene has yet been identified that is specific to growth or the development of emotional systems" (Panksepp [1998], 319).

33. Kosfeld, et al, 673.

34. Benzon, 81.

35. Nelson, Haan, and Thomas, 39. "[T]here are new ample data to suggest that learning and memory are connected with changes in the brain at multiple levels, from changes in pre- and post-synaptic functioning mediated by glutamate receptors to the motor changes at the level of anatomy." Further, they note: "There is little or no evidence to suggest a sensitive period for learning and memory to occur. . . . Indeed, there is some sense that activities that engage the learning and memory system may confer some protection on lifelong learning and memory function" (39-40).

36. Damasio, 198-199. Demasio points out that "optics stop at the retna," that is, images from the outside end when they are transposed into neural circuits" (200).

37. *Ibid.*, 199, emph. add. Kandel and Schwartz write: "Behavioral and electrophysiological experiments suggest that short term sensitization grades into long-term sensitization" (Kandel and Schwartz [1982], 438-439).

38. "The ensemble of sensory detectors are located throughout our bodies and help construct neural patterns that map the comprehensive *interaction* of the organism with the object along its many dimensions" (Demasio, 199).

39. Demasio, 199, 200.

40. Kandel and Schwartz write: "With respected sensory stimulation at rates that produce habituation in the intact animal, the neurosynaptic excitatory connections between the sensory and motor neurons are functionally depressed because less transmitter is released by each impulse in the sensory neurons. Transmitter at chemical synapses is related in molecular packets called quanta. An analysis of habituation in

terms of the quantal components of synaptic transmission indicates that, in this form of learning, fewer transmitter quanta are released from the terminals by each action potential. [The sensitivity of the receptor molecules in the postsynaptic cells is not altered.] Similarly, sensitization produces pre-synaptic (heterosynaptic) facilitation at the terminals of the sensory neurons by increasing the number of transmitter quante released per impulse. Thus the amount of transmitter released by sensory cells is modulated in opposite ways by habituation and sensitization" (Kandel and Schwartz [1982], 434).

41. Giulio Tononi and Gerald Edelman, "Consciousness and Complexity," *Essential Sources in the Scientific Study of Consciousness*, eds. Bernard Baurs, William Bowls, and James Newman (Cambridge, MA: MIT UP, 2003), 996, 995-966.

42. Dolan and Morris add: "organisms have to contend with unpredictable environments, and mechanisms that signal novel behavior that enhance adaptive fitness are important" (Dolan and Morris, 232).

43. Kandel and Schwartz (1982), 441; LeDoux (1996), 213. For more on the various theories of learning and memory, see: Endel Tulving, "Memory and Consciousness," *Essential Sources in the Scientific Study of Consciousness*, ed. Bernard Baurs, William Bowls, and James Newman (Cambridge, MA: MIT UP, 2003): 579-591; Arthur Reber, "Implicit Learning and Tacit Knowledge" in *Essential Sources in the Scientific Study of Consciousness*, 603-630; Richard Shiffrin, "Attention, Automatism, and Consciousness," in *Essential Sources in the Scientific Study of Consciousness*, 631-654; Marcus Raichte, "The Neural Correlates of Conscious: An Analysis of Cognitive Skill Learning," in *Essential Sources in the Scientific Study of Consciousness*, 654-675; John Gerdiner, Christina Ramponi, and Alan Richardson-Klarehin, "Experiences of Remembering, Knowing, and Guessing," in *Essential Sources in the Scientific Study of Consciousness*, 697-720; and Stephen Grossberg, "Brain Learning, Attention, and Consciousness," in *Essential Sources in the Scientific Study of Consciousness*, 1007-1034.

44. Kandel and Schwartz (1982), 439; LeDoux (1996), 216; Kandel and Pittenger, (1999) 2035; Eric Kandel, "Genes, Nerve Cells, and the Remembrance of Things Past," *Journal of Neuropsychiatry* 1.2 (1999): 103-125. Hogue explains: "Postsynaptic cells apparently have ways to recognize the specific cells that trigger the responses—that is, to "remember" them—to that they won't fire in response to just any old cell" (Hogue, 64).

45. Freeman (1997), 68. Eric Kandel explains more specifically: "Memory storage for explicit [long-term] forms of knowing requires structures within the temporal lobe including the hippocampus. The hippocampus itself has 3 major and a number of minor) synaptic relays in a series. Input to the hippocampus comes from the neurons of the entorhinal cortex by means of their axons, the perforant pathway, that synapse on the granule cells of the dentate gyrus. The granule cells in turn send their axons, the mossy fiber pathway, to synapse on the pyramidal cells of the CA3 region. Finally, the axons of the pyramidal cells in the CA3 regions, the Schaffer collateral pathway, terminate on the pyramidal cells of the CA1 region. Each of these pathways makes a direct monosynaptic connection on its target cells, and damage to a single pathway within the hippocampus is sufficient to produce memory disturbance in humans" (Eric Kandel, "Genes, Synapses, and Long-Term Memory," *Journal of Cellular Physiology* 173 [1997], 124). Cf. Daniel Schacter, Nathaniel Alpert, Carry Savage, Scott Rauch, and Marilyn Albert, "Conscious Recollection and the Human Hippocampal Formation," in *Essential Sources in the Scientific Study of* Consciousness, eds. Bernard Baurs, William Bowls, and James Newman (Cambridge, MA: MIT UP, 2003): 594-601.

46. Freeman (1997), 68; cf. Kandel (1976), 494. Dolan and Morris: "The Specific predictions regarding the neural processes that mediate acquired value or salience involve an increase in the strength of inputs from. . . processing systems, engaged by particular adaptive behaviors, to the value systems themselves. Consequently, neural patterns that antecede value-related behaviors become capable of eliciting a response in value systems. At a mechanistic level this involves an increase in the strength of afferents from sensory systems to the value systems involving neuromodulartory-medicated plasticity" (Dolan and Morris, 232-233).

47. Demasio, 200. Demasio continues: "It should not be surprising that similar images arise out of those similar neural patterns [between different people]. That is why we can accept, without protest, the conventional idea that each of us has formed in our minds the reflected picture of some particular thing. In reality we did not" (200).

48. LeDoux (2002), 324.

49. Cf. Damasio, 6. Clearly, we could splice differences between "feelings" and emotions—which may, on a philosophical level, bear some fruit. For the time being, however, I will focus on presenting a few theories of emotion to inform our later theological discussion.

50. "Complex organisms also learn to modulate the execution of emotions in harmony wih the individual circumstances. . . . The emotional modulation devices can adjust the magnitude of emotional expression without an organism's deliberation" (Demasio, 56).

51. d'Aquili, Newberg, and Rouse (2001), 51-52. The authors continue: "The existential operator most likely resides, in part at least, in the limbic system, since emotion is such an important part of all real experiences. But our sense of things being real also requires sensory elements—we need to touch, hear, smell, taste, and, of course, see things before we can judge them as real—so it is probable that the existential operator also derives some of its function from the sensory association areas" (52).

52. *Ibid.* (2001), 52.

53. *Ibid.* 52, 53. They write, further: "every event that happens to us or any action that we take can be associated with activity in one or more specific regions of the brain. This includes, necessarily, all religious and spiritual experiences. The evidence further compels us to believe that if God does indeed exist, the only place he can manifest his existence would be in the tangled neural pathways and physiological structures of the brain" (53).

54. Panksepp (1998), 309. Further: Neurodynamic ripples of various affective codes may spread widely through the brain. The interaction of these neurodynamics with the sensory analyzers of the thalamus and cortex and the motor systems they regulate allows organisms the possibility of various species-typical modes of emotional SELF-expression and SELF-regulation" (309).

55. *Ibid.*

56. Thandeka (2005), 213.

57. Panksepp (1998), 309, emph. add. Panksepp continues on this point: "According to the present argument (i.e., that a neural entity such as 'the SELF" does exist in the brain), the bottom-line statement probably should be 'I am, therefore I am.' In any event, we probably should not persist in chastising Descartes for giving primacy to 'I think, therefore I am.' In *The Passions of the Soul*, Descartes did accept the primacy of emotion

in experience, but for perhaps political reasons (to avoid religious persecution, to which Galileo suffered) he drew a strict dualistic line between bodily processes (which included emotions) and mind/soul processes (which included thoughts)" (420 n.34.).

58. *Ibid.* 420 n. 34.
59. *Ibid.* 318.
60. *Ibid.*, emph. add.
61. *Ibid.*, de-emphasized. He continues: "Such a primitive SELF-representation presumably consists of an intrinsically reverberating neural network linked to basic body tone and gross axial movement generators. . . . When other incoming stimuli, both internal and external, interact with this body schema and establish new kinds of different reverberations, the potential for an internal state of affective awareness is created. Obviously, for such an entity to have adaptive value, it must be able to control certain basic motor functions and attitudinal processes" (310).
62. *Ibid.*, 309, 319. Thandeka summarizes well Panksepp's framework for the neural basis of our affections into six steps:

1. *The feeling of experiencing oneself in the world=a feeling.*
2. *This feeling is a self-representation.*
3. *This self representation refers to a pattern of neural. . . circuitry (with its discrete anatomical, chemical, and physiological patterning characteristics).*
4. *This feeling represents an overall neural state of the organism.*
5. *This state is an affective state of consciousness of the organism known as a mood, disposition, or emotion.*
6. *This feeling, as the dominant state, is the first representation of the body as an "intrinsic and coherent whole." It is a body schema, a neural pattern that expresses a system of systems as a disposition, personality, or character trait.*
7. *When this feeling is altered by new internal or external neural patterns, "the potential for an internal state of affective awareness is created."* (Thandeka [2005], 213, partially quoting Panksepp, from Panksepp [1998], 310n. 30).

63. Jaak Panksepp, "The Emotional Sources of 'Chills' Induced by Music," *Music Perception* 13.2 (1995), 203; Émile Durkheim, *Durkheim on Religion*, ed. W. Pickering (Atlanta: Scholars, 1994), 128-130, 135-136, and 253-254; Mihaly Csilszentmihali, *Flow: The Psychology of Optimal Experience* (Grand Rapids, MI: Harper, 1990); cf. Marghanita Laski, *Ecstasy: A Study of Some Secular and Religious Experiences* (Bloomington, IN: Indiana UP, 1961), esp. 317ff.; Alf Gabrielson, "Emotions in Strong Experiences with Music," *Music and Emotion: Theory and Research*, ed. Patrik Jaslin and John Sloboda (Oxford, England: Oxford UP, 2001), 431-449.
64. Abraham Maslow, *Motivation and Personality*, 2nd ed., ed. Wayne Holtzman and Gardner Murphy (New York: Harper, 1970), 164-165.
65. Robert Panzarella, "The Phenomenology of Aesthetic Peak Experiences," *Journal of Humanistic Psychology* 20.1 (1980), 70; Csikszentmihalyi, 67. Csikszentmihalyi contrasts autotelic experiences to "exotelic" experiences, which are activities that may be enjoyable but clearly have a clear purpose. For example, teaching children, certainly a noble cause, appears to be an immediately exotelic activity, since one might teach children out of enjoyment, a sense of social justice, or for some other reason (Csikszentmihalyi, 67).

66. Gabrielson 432; Abraham Maslow, *Toward a Psychology of Being*, 2nd ed. (New York: Van Nostrand Reinhold, 1968), 87-88. Gabrielson: "[p]eak experience is good and desireable, there is a complete loss of fear, anxiety, inhibition, defense, and control" (431).

67. *Ibid.*, 432, citing Laski.

68. Maslow (1968), 88. Gabrielson: peaking involves a "total attention to the object in question, complete absorption, disorientation in time and space, transcendence of ego, and identification or even fusion of the perceiver and perceived" (Gabrielson, 431).

69. Panzarella 78. Cf. Karl Rahner and Karl Vorgrimler, *Theological Dictionary*, trans. Richard Strachan, ed. Cornelius Ernst (New York: Herder, 1965), 223.

70. Panzarella, 70, drawing heavily on Maslow's research.

71. Panksepp (1995), 178; Gabrielson, 432; Panzarella, 76.

72. Panzarella, 76, 75, 77. Interestingly, visual experience accounts more for "renewal ecstasy"—38%, opposed to 14% for musical experience (75)—and music is associated more strongly for the "fusion-emotional ecstasy"—27%, as opposed to 17% for visual experience (77).

73. Panksepp (1995), 183, 185, 195.

74. *Ibid.*, 189. For more on the neurological basis of music or auditory experiences: B. Hars, C. Maho, J. Edeline, and E. Hennevin, "Basal Forebrain Stimulation Facilitates Tone-Evoked Responses in the Auditory Cortex of Awake Rat," *Neuroscience* 56.1 (1993): 51-74; Isabelle Peretz, "Listen to the Brain: A Biological Perspective on Musical Emotions," *Music and Emotion*, eds. Patrik Jaslin and John Sloboda (Oxford, England: Oxford UP, 2001): 105-134.

75. Panksepp (1995), 203.

76. Panzarella, 78-79; cf. Gilbert Rouget, *Music and Trance*, trans. and rev. Brunhilde Biebuyck (Chicago: U Chicago P, 1985).

77. Gabrielson, 432, 433..

78. Ornstein, 122.

79. Panksepp (1998), 309.

80. Csikszentmihalyi, 68. Another separate theory of emotion and feeling, attributed to Joseph LeDoux, which focuses its attention to the converging synchronicity of brain systems as defining pathways toward memory and learning, and the notion that emotional states limit the brain's ability to interpret and respond to the world. LeDoux's theory is not extraordinarily different than those theories explored here, but is perhaps a different way of explaining similar concepts—and it has been enormously influential within the field of neurotheology. For more, see LeDoux (2002), 308-324; J. Feit 10-13; and Carol Albright, "Religious Experience, Complexification, and the Image of God," *NeuroTheology: Brain, Science, Spirituality, Religious Experience*, ed. R. Joseph (San Jose, CA: University Press, 2003), esp. 175-176.

81. Cf. Csikszentmihalyi, 108-109, 111. John Sloboda and Susan O'Neill: "Although viewed as essentially 'private' experiences, including a great deal of autonomy or agency, emotional feelings and displays are deeply embedded in a social context, when exerts a powerful influence (albeit often implicitly) on our music listening. Reliving past relationships, constructing identity. . . all of these depend on, and are used to negotiate and develop, the complex web of cognitions and behaviours [*sic*.] that constitute social life." Continuing: "As such, music becomes part of the construction of

emotional feelings, and displays that are both reflective and communicative 'embodied' judgments used to accomplish particular social acts. In other words, musical emotions are a form of *social* representation, which is negotiated as an intersection between cultural/ideological values of a society, the values and beliefs operating in a social grouping or subculture in that society, and the individuals own social and personal experience" (John Sloboda and Susan O'Neill, "Emotions in Everyday Listening to Music," *Music and Emotion*, eds. Patrik Jaslin and John Sloboda [Oxford, England: Oxford UP, 2001] 427). Cf. Mark Wynn, "Musical Affects and the Life of Faith," *Faith and Philosophy* 21 (2004): 25-44.

82. Cf. Damasio, 7.

Chapter Four
The Neurology of Worship

We have explored in the previous chapter the scientific belief that feelings are rooted in a physiological configuration of our brains. Furthermore, emotions and feelings may be said, in philosophical terms, to be the means by which we *engage the world*: emotions allow our brains to respond, cope, and adapt to the changing realities of the world around us.[1] It is for this reason that, as an example, I may speak of having had a very different experience—one of abjection and grief—while watching the film, *The Passion of the Christ*, in the local movie theater, while the stranger sitting next to me obviously had a deeply moving experience during the film, weeping and instinctually uttering prayers of gratitude to Christ throughout the movie. We both came to the film from different places, from different gendered and cultural perspectives, probably from different economic conditions, and these *social* entrenchments that we carry are actualized in the way that our brains are wired. As such, we experienced seemingly contrary emotions while experiencing the same film.[2]

To employ a similar example: I remember watching the film *The Deer Hunter* on television when I was in sixth or seventh grade, and I was frightened, appalled, and shocked by a sequence in the film where Vietnamese military men gambled over American prisoners of war forced into playing Russian roulette. Later in the film, a character commits suicide while voluntarily playing Russian roulette for gambling profits.[3] I had nightmares for weeks during these prepubescent years as a response to the movie. Years later, when I watched *The Deer Hunter* with some friends in college, I distinctively recalled the abjection of watching before, but this time I had a deeper appreciation for the film as a work of art. Despite the fact that the film had not changed, and the content of the film was no less disturbing than it was ten years before, *I* had changed. I was older; I had learned to interpret art differently; I had learned to negotiate or suppress my emotions differently; I had become less shocked by violence (and, perhaps, *habituated* into violence in the popular culture that I consumed); and I was, in fact, then living near the part of Pennsylvania where significant scenes of *The Deer Hunter* had taken place. I had changed, and my contexts had changed.

Ritual theorist Catherine Bell writes that "human activity is situational, which is to say that much of what is important to it cannot be grasped outside of the specific context in which it occurs."[4] As such, we can experience the same or similar things very differently at different points in our lives: as a child we may approach Disney World with a sense of wonder, joy, anticipation, and play; as a young adult academic I approach Disney World with a sense of suspicion and resentment for its capitalism, colonialism, and materialistic escapism; as a parent of a young child I anticipate experiencing Disney World for the wonder, joy, anticipation, and play of my child.[5] We experience the world with the totality of our past experiences and present realities: a *totality* of experience that is constantly changing and often contradictory. Everything that happens to us is molded, shaped, and interpreted by our brains; our brains cope with new experiences by making sense of them within the reality in which we live and know.[6] New experiences can also push our brains to *plastically* grow, change, or *negate* old systems as we are challenged. We become *habituated* into our ritualistic patterns of behavior, until something changes the patterns, and then we habituate into something new, as D. Winnicott writes, "the task of reality acceptance is never completed."[7]

THE "IMMEDIACY OF INTERPRETATION" AND POSITIVE MOODS

In this ever-engaged and engaging human condition, we live in what philosopher John Russon calls "the immediacy of interpretation." In our perpetual habituating and coping-with-reality, which is always changing, Russon writes, "we exist interpretively." Whether we interpret from a positive or negative mood (or *mostly* positive or *mostly* negative moods) is a "fundamental way in which interpretive experience is experienced by us."[8] Since worship is something that can *construct* reality, worship may help us taint our experience of the world positively or negatively.

Our brain circuitry is wired to be negative when not intentionally trying to be positive. According to psychologists Rollin McCraty and Doc Childre, "[i]n the absence of conscious efforts to engage, build, and sustain positive perceptions and emotions, we all too automatically fall prey to feelings such as irritation, anxiety, worry, frustration, judgmentalness, self-doubt, and blame." If our lives are overly negative, these negative emotions and mood patterns become "reinforced" in our synaptic circuitry, thereby making a negative worldview "increasingly automatic and mechanical." To this end, McCraty and

Childre add that "[m]any people do not realize the extent to which these habitual response patterns dominate their internal landscape, *diluting* and *limiting positive emotional experience* and eventually becoming so familiar that they become *engraved* in one's sense of self-identity."[9] Thinking immediately of a character from A. A. Milne's Winnie-the-Pooh book series (as well as in the Disney films), Eeyore is a gray donkey who has a completely negative outlook on life, to the point that he lives in an area called "Eeyore's Gloomy Place" and eats thistles.[10] We have all experienced individuals, like Eeyore, who are seemingly unable to *feel* themselves out of their own negativity; they act the way they do largely because they have been *habituated* into negative patterns.

Positive moods and emotions not only color our interpretive experiences of the world, but they also lead to more positive emotions, such as gratitude or pride.[11] Furthermore, positive emotions are believed to "broaden the scope of cognition and enable flexible and creative thinking," as well as "facilitate coping with stress and adversity." For example, a study of individuals following a death close to them, who had intentionally sought out positive emotions around the time of the death "were much more likely to develop long-term plans and goals," which led them to have "greater psychological well-being twelve months after bereavement." Barbara Fredrickson writes in response:

> Thus, the effects of positive emotions appear to accumulate and compound over time. These emotions not only make people feel good in the present, but they also increase the likelihood that people will function well and feel good in the future. By broadening people's modes of thinking and action, positive emotions improve coping and build resilience, improvements that in turn predict future experiences of positive emotions.[12]

According to McCraty and Childre, "positive thinking" must also occur with "positive feelings" for long-term change to occur.[13]

One positive emotion that is often associated with religious experience is gratitude; nearly every major world religious tradition places a heavy emphasis upon gratitude.[14] In a study of Catholic nuns and priests, gratitude and love were cited as "the most frequent of fifty distinct emotions felt toward God."[15] Gratitude may be understood as a two-step process: first, "recognizing that one has obtained a positive outcome," and second, "recognizing that there is an external source for this positive outcome." Beyond these, to experience gratitude requires one to observe that one's "positive outcome" is not an entitlement, and is something others do not have; as such, gratitude is an emotion "whose roots lie in the capacity to empathize with others."[16] What's more, psychologists Dan McAdams and Jack Bauer suggest that gratitude may function—from an evolutionary perspective—as the means by which individuals successfully integrate and differentiate within groups.[17]

Positive emotions arise within groups or in conjunction with others, as opposed to occurring in an isolated or solipsistic state. This may be attributed to the fact that many positive emotions (empathy, gratitude, acceptance, etc.) *require others*: social interaction, for most people, "generally feels good." Communities can experience emotions together, since, as Barbara Fredrickson writes, "each persons' positive emotions can reverberate through others;" positive emotions or moods are "contagious." Positive emotions can even be transmitted, as is easily observed with infants, through our faces; just as one baby crying will often lead to a second one crying in a very primal form of empathy.[18]

The emotions of a group's leader can be particularly affective; researchers "have shown. . . that a leader's positive emotion [can] predict the performance of the entire group." Beyond this, *positive* group leaders not only transmit *positive* moods, but the leaders' own positive moods for themselves will often lead to *self-affirming* actions. As a result, a positive leader has the potential to create a "chain of events that carry positive meaning for others" within a group who hold similar or overlapping interpretive realities.[19]

Our neural architecture's circuitry associates different moods or emotions within different communities or localities. If my experience of my extended family is limited to funerals or family tragedies, for example, then I will primarily associate that familial community with those feelings encountered there, even if I am generally positive at other times with other groups. If our experience of church is solemn or being bored, then church experiences will typically be associated with solemnity or boredom. Or our experiences could be rooted in a *desire for what happens when we depart church*, based upon *hunger:* longing for the weekly family meal after church, which we may associate with positive emotions. We are creatures of *habit*, and we *habituate* as individuals and as part of groups.

THEORIES OF HABITUATION

Throughout our discussions the words "habit" and "habituation" have emerged numerous times; this is because psychologists, neural physiologists, and philosophers have all used these terms to describe the patterns and homogeneities that our lives and interpretations of reality take.[20] Psychologist Philip Watkins describes a "law of habituation" as the fact that "we get used to our current level of satisfaction"—that is, on a very basic level, we do not explicitly enact or wish for change in our lives' patterns and routines.[21] Going back to ancient philosophy, Aristotle writes in his *Nicomachean Ethics*:

> Virtue. . . being of two kinds, intellectual and moral, intellectual virtue in the main owes both its birth and its growth to teaching (for which reason it requires experience and time), while moral virtue comes about as a result of *habit*, whence also its name is one that is formed by a slight variation from the word

ethos (habit). From this it is also plain that none of the moral virtues arises in us by nature; for nothing that exists by nature can form a habit contrary to its nature.

Aristotle then offers an example in rather pedestrian terms:

> For instance the stone which by nature moves downwards cannot be *habituated* to move upwards, not even if one tries to train it by throwing it up ten thousand times; nor can fire be habituated to move downwards, nor can anything else that by nature behaves in one way to be trained to behave in another. Neither by nature, then, nor contrary to nature do the virtues arise in us; rather we are *adapted* by nature to receive them, and we are made perfect by habit.[22]

To make another concrete example, Aristotle famously suggests that "the things we have to learn before we can do them, we learn before we can do them, we learn by doing them, e.g. men become builders by building and lyre-players by playing the lyre; so too we become just by doing just acts, temperate by doing temperate acts, brave by doing brave acts."[23] In other words, we learn by doing, and learning-by-doing is a way to learn a new musical instrument inasmuch as it is a way of being a good person. Aristotle philosophizes the point that I wish to make: our habits (*ethos*) are related to our emotions or moods, and are thus related to our characters or dispositions, which are finally related to our values and individual constructions of reality.

But, as we have seen, habits begin within us on a neural level. Neurologist Eric Kandel calls habituation a "decrease in the amplitude of a progressive reflex response when the response is repeatedly elicited."[24] Habituation, then, is not a *strengthening* of neural synaptic connections, but rather, it is a "weakening" or "sensitizing" of neural pathways and connections.[25] As a weakening impulse, whetting us into new neural pathways, habituation underlies much of learning and memory, as discussed in an earlier chapter.[26] Psychologist Robert Ornstein describes habituation with a phenomenon he calls the "Bowrey El effect." He explains:

> An elevated railroad once ran along Third Avenue in New York City. At a certain time, late each night, a noisy train ran. The train line was torn down some time ago, with some interesting after-effects. Many people in the neighborhood called the police to report "something strange" occurring late at night—noises, thieves, burglars, etc. The police determined that those calls took place around the time of the former late-night train. What those people were "hearing," of course, was the *absence* of the familiar noise of the train.[27]

Ornstein concludes that the "'Bowrey El effect'. . . suggests that we tune out the recurrences of the world by making a 'model' of the external world within our nervous system[s], and testing input against it." This demonstrates how our habituations are in fact *interpretive*, and how our habituations locate us as *subjective* individuals approaching the same reality *differently*. Our "assumptive worlds" may—and often *do*—*trick* us, while constructing reality.[28]

Critical philosopher Pierre Bourdieu, in his social philosophy works, refers to the idea of *habitus*, which he says, is "history turned into nature."[29] *Habitus* is the *collective history* of the whole of our interpretations of reality from our beginnings, compiled—or perhaps *compiling* and *collapsing*—onto our "immediacy of interpretation" in the present. It is the means by which our interpretive selves (that is, our "SELVES") adapt or reconcile our habits around socially- or culturally-constructed experiences, such as public festivals or holidays. *Habitus*, however, in turn leads us to "homogeneity," *ritualizing* us into patterns and the danger of taking our daily, day-to-day experiences for granted.[30] It is, in essence, our "internal law."[31]

Phenomenological philosopher John Russon calls habituation a process by which "we accustom ourselves to sophisticated modes of contacting" other objects, experiences, and people, "and the key to something becoming habitual is that it makes a more sophisticated action possible by making its own primitive behavior automatic and inconspicuous."[32] Habits, then, "are structures of *repression*, structures in which we refuse to acknowledge what we are actually doing; indeed, develop this refusal to the point that recognition of what we are doing is not in our power." As a *repression* (that is, "an occlusion of vision"), "the structure of habit is still very much a structure of memory. . . it is the most *fundamental* remembering, a *remembering* that is precisely a *forgetting*."[33] Russon explains further in a long paragraph:

> We can have reflective memory by engaging in a present act of explicating the significance that is latent in the objects of our experience, but our implicit and pervasive remembering is the experiencing as a familiar immediacy the habitual figures we have developed for interpreting—interacting with—our situation. We become habituated to structures of recollection and anticipation, which is to say that we commit ourselves to certain narratives about what we will recognize as the *determinacy* of our situation and what we project on its horizon. It is *as* the *determinacy* of our situation that this repressed structure of anticipation and recollection is remembered.[34]

"Determinacy," for Russon, is a psychological and physiological ability to say "I can" to experiences in the world. For example:

> If. . . one has become habituated to coping with one's interpersonal life through fighting (if, say, that is the only way one's parents would allow one to have what one desires) then it is in terms of the demands of a fighting life that one will view situations. If one has become habituated to fighting over how one must eat one's dinner, then one may find that one often feels despondent around dinner time, or when placed with plates and cutlery. This immediate feeling would be an implicit remembering that "I will now be refused" or

something similar. Or, again, an innocent question from a friend during a meal may be experienced as a threatening feeling of transgression against which one must protect oneself.

"In such ways," Russon concludes, "our developed moods are the immediate presentation of how we believe we should 'expect' based on habitual commitments."[35]

Through habituation, then, we increase the *determinacy*—that is, the "bodily 'I can'"—by which we approach the world. Through this *process* of habituation, Russon writes, "[t]he world and its constituent objects are fundamentally structures of the memory and the forms of this 'I can' and its habituation and development into a familiar 'being-at-home' as a stable person in a stable setting." As such, habituation is a *process* through which we bring the exigency of the past—*our* own pasts—into the present. Finally, for Russon, habituation is a *process* that leads to becoming "stable selves-in-the-world."[36]

Like Jaak Pankseep's conception of "the SELF" (as discussed in the previous chapter), within Russon's conception of habituation is a fundamental inner principle that *determines* our ability to experience the world. Furthermore, this inner principle allows or disallows us from fully experiencing the world or from experiencing the world in healthy ways. Finally, this inner principle is a means by which we might assert the self in meaningful—and perhaps *liberative*—ways in the world that we experience. Through a healthy determinacy to say "I can" to the world, our habituations may be *dishabituated* to form new habituations; if an individual's determinacy is reluctant to say "I can" to new realities in one's experienced world.[37]

Along with our determinacies and abilities to experience the world, our value systems are also habituated. Aristotle speculated long ago that habits require practice: as mentioned earlier, an excellent musician requires not just some practice, but a great deal of practice, mistakes, and even *self-sacrifices* all lead to excellence. For Aristotle, the same is also true for our virtues and values. We have to learn and experience the world, and we must continue to experience the more of the world, or experience the world more richly and deeply, to truly continue to habituate and dishabituate our habituations. If our determinacies limit our habituations—that is, to "say no" to expanding our experiences or "I can't" to experiencing the world further, rather than an "I can"—the ability to find excellence in our virtues may be limited. Through the expansion of our experiences, the broader our habituations and our abilities to habituate, and the healthier our determanicies, the more rich our daily, banal, *ritualized* patterns might become. Furthermore, our behaviors will also become more indicative or integral to our habituations.[38]

HABITUATION AND RITUAL

Ritual and public worship[*] have the ability to be formative, community-building and self-actualizing experiences to individuals. This is more true for children, youth, and young adults, whose moral, spiritual, and neurological development is at its greatest potential during the younger years.[39] What habituates us ritualistically into communities is the repetition of words, prayers, songs, liturgical forms and expectations, bodily movements, smells, stories and spaces for storytelling, and so on. My perspective is that for worship to be habituative a *strict* liturgical *order* does not need to be maintained, but rather, the *space* for liturgical experience and empathy to occur should be repeated, affirmed, and performed.[40]

The repetition of certain prayers and liturgical experiences, however, does seem to have some habitual benefit. d'Aquili and Newberg write that "slow rhythmicity seems to drive the quiescent system to increasing intensity while 'rapid' rhythmicity seems to drive the arousal system to ever increasing intensity." In other words, on a neurological level, regarding rhythmic repetition, a neural system's ability to "take in" the experience, using d'Aquili and Newberg's words, "spill over" or "erupt" into another system.[41] Following this neurological paradigm, they offer the following definition of ritual. Ritual is a "sequence of behavior" that fits the following conditions:

1. Ritual is structured or patterned;
2. is rhythmic and repetitive (to some degree at least), that is, tends to recur in the same or nearly the same form with some regularity;
2. acts to synchronize affective, perceptual-cognitive, and motor processes within the central nervous system of individual participants; and
3. most particularly, synchronizes these processes among the various individual participants.[42]

This suggests that ritual, if it is not affective on a neurological level, is ineffective. While this definition might seem to be a difficult check-list of "things to do" for public worship, I believe that these basic principles of conditions occur on subtle levels in typical Christian worship.

I will offer some examples. Many of my Roman Catholic friends, for example, describe the scent of the incense used in their worship services—as part of a processional, the Eucharistic ritual, or even the blessing of a coffin in a Catholic funeral—acts as an aromatic indicator that "it's time for worship," "we now encounter the holy," or even triggers a muscular relaxation. From my own

---

[*] I use the term *public worship* here to distinguish against private religious practices, which I believe function differently on a variety of levels, including the neurological level (cf. d'Aquili and Newberg [1999], 5-6, 13).

pastoral experience, I have encountered numerous individuals in hospitals or nursing homes, who, while in an unconscious or unawake state, would begin to speak or their lips would move—or in one case, the patient woke up temporarily—during the Lord's Prayer or the Apostle's Creed. I have officiated numerous funerals or weddings with individuals who would not consider themselves religious or have not attended a public worship service for years, but make the sign of the cross with their hand after certain signals or phrases (such as "in the name of the Father, and the Son, and the Holy Spirit"). Repeated rituals—that only employ words or simple movements—habituate us into worshiping together, into being community.[43]

Walter Freeman has argued that ritual is at its best, which is to say, contributes to our adaptation (self-actualizing, liberative changes, etc.), through oxytocin, the neuro-peptide discussed in an earlier chapter.[44] To recall, oxytocin is believed to be a key element in the changing of neural synaptic connections and is associated to familial attachment in animals. Freeman writes:

> Scientists have learned that, when animals mate and give birth, specialized chemicals are released into their brains that enable their behavior to change. Maternal and paternal patterns of nursing and caring appear. The most important is a chemical called 'oxytocin.' It doesn't cause joy. On the contrary, it may cause anxiety, because it melts down the patterns of connections among neurons that hold experience, so that new experience can form. We become aware of this meltdown most dramatically as a frightening loss of identity of self control, when we fall in love for the first time. Bonding comes not with the meltdown, but with the shared activity afterward, in which people learn about each other through cooperation. . . .
>
> Oxytocin is not a happiness chemical, but a brain tool for building trust. Perhaps a million years ago our ancestors learned how to use the mammalian mechanism to promote social bonding beyond sexual union, in order to form groups and tribes. They did it, and still do it, with dancing, rhythmic clapping and chanting, singing, making music together all day and night, often into exhaustion and collapse. When they awaken, they are reborn.[45]

Oxytocin, then, is a chemical that is associated with familial intimacy and community; Freeman suggests that rhythmic drumming and action *re-creates*, in groups, the rhythmic intimacy of sexual union and natal experience of joining and rejoining with the mother. Oxytocin does not create this experience, but, according to Freeman, it opens us up to the experience.[46] It "attunes" individuals' nervous systems for the possibility of the individual to enter into a larger community or group of people.[47]

William Benzon explains Freeman's hypothesis as follows. "As the oxytoxinated individuals move to the rhythms of well-established ritual," he explains, "their synaptic connections are restructured in patterns guided and influenced by the events of the ritual." In turn, the "rituals provide a space in which individuals can mold themselves to one another as the infant molds her actions to those of her mother."[48] To be sure, rituals are not necessarily about an actual *return* to the mother, but rather, *rituals build intimate communities among those who are not necessarily related by blood*—perhaps, as an example, bringing exigency to the presence and ritual significance of the font as the ecclesiastical cervix or womb of the church as a symbol for a need to be "born anew" or "again." Benzon further explains that for Freeman, "[t]he social purpose [of oxytocin] lies in better interpersonal relations, while the cultural mechanism, of course, is the ritual activity." Furthermore, since oxytocin weakens synaptic connections, its "biological process is. . . to dissolve or weaken interpersonal bonds so that they can be 'reset' along lines carved in the ritual and in subsequent activity." The symbolic bath of baptism in the font (often with a clamshell, a symbol of the feminine) is, especially in evangelical Protestant traditions, a necessary starting-over, a *rebirth* into the community of believers. That said, the biological function of oxytocin, for Freeman, leads us to its social significance for ritual.[49]

CONCLUSION

Rituals are not only a means by which we worship, nor even just a catalyst for self-actualization, but they are a set of habituated "dispositions" which define our social realities with the world and others. As such, rituals habituate us into a "socially informed body," with "all of its *senses*;" and "effects a *fluid, 'fuzzy' abstraction*," creating symbols and meaning-making into liturgical speech, action, and sense.[50] To this end, Aidan Kavanagh calls liturgy an "ecclesial transaction with reality," that is, "a transaction whose ramifications escape over the horizons of the present, beyond the act itself, to overflow even the confines of the local assembly into universality."[51] In other words, rituals have the power to construct reality around us, create communities or intimacy between people where there was none prior, and even push us into a greater empathy for those outside of the community's boundaries. But we must first be *open* to the possible habituation that rituals provide to us.[52]

NOTES: CHAPTER FOUR

1. Robert Solomon, "Emotion, Thoughts, and Feelings: Emotions as Engagements with the World," *Thinking About Feeling: Contemporary Philosophers on Emotions*, ed. Robert Solomon (New York: Oxford UP, 2004), 76-77ff.

2. Cf. Annette Baier, "Feelings that Matter," *Thinking About Feeling: Contemporary Philosophers on Emotions*, ed. Robert Solomon (New York: Oxford UP, 2004), 200; *The Passion of the Christ* (2004) was famously directed my Mel Gibson.

3. *The Deer Hunter* (1978) was directed by Michael Cimino.

4. Catherine Bell, *Ritual Theory, Ritual Practice* (New York: Oxford UP, 1992), 81.

5. Cf. Jon Pahl, Shopping Malls and Other Sacred Spaces (Grand Rapids, MI: Brazos, 2003); Christopher Rodkey, Review of *Shopping Malls and Other Sacred Spaces, Journal of Cultural and Religious Theory* (2004): 147-149.

6. Michael Lerner, *Surplus Powerlessness: The Psychodynamics of Everyday Life. . . and the Psychology of Individual and Social Transformation* (Atlantic Highlands, NJ: Humanities Press International, 1991), 62.

7. D. Winnicott, *Playing and Reality* (London: Tavistock/Routledge, 1991), 13.

8. John Russon, *Human Experience: Philosophy, Neurosis, and the Elements of Everyday Life* (Albany, NY: SUNY UP, 2003), 45.

9. McCraty and Childre, 241-242, emph. add.

10. See, for example, A. A. Milne's *The House at Pooh Corner* (London: Methuen, 1928).

11. Michael McCullough and Jo-Ann Tsung, "Parent of the Virtues?", *The Psychology of Gratitude*, ed. Robert Emmons and Michael McCullough (New York: Oxford UP, 2004), 127.

12. Barbara Fredrickson, "Gratitude, Like Other Positive Emotions, Broadens and Builds," *The Psychology of Gratitude*, ed. Robert Emmons and Michael McCullough (New York: Oxford UP, 2004), 153, 155.

13. McCraty and Childre, 242.

14. Fredrickson, 152; cf. Solomon Schimmel, "Gratitude in Judaism," *Psychology of Gratitude*, ed. Robert Emmons and Michael McCullough (New York: Oxford UP, 2004), 39ff.

15. Fredrickson 151, citing Samuels and Lester, 706.

16. Robert Emmons, "The Psychology of Gratitude," *The Psychology of Gratitude*, ed. Robert Emmons and Michael McCullough (New York: Oxford UP, 2004), 9.

17. Dan McAdams and Jack Bauer, "Gratitude in Modern Life," *The Psychology of Gratitude*, ed. Robert Emmons and Michael McCullough (New York: Oxford UP, 2004), 86. They continue on this point: "the individual who is capable of gratitude, who is blessed with the propensity to engage with others in gracious ways, may find that his or her standing in the group is ultimately enhanced, contributing ultimately to inclusive fitness. Put simply, the capacity to experience and express gratitude in groups may give an individual an adaptive advantage, positioning him or her well for survival and reproductive opportunities in life. Gratitude may be grouped, therefore, in the same family as kin selection and reciprocated altruism-evolved adaptations that have proven so useful for fitness in group living that they have become, more or less, foundational features of human nature" (86).

18. Fredrickson, 157.

19. *Ibid.* 157, citing Jennifer George, "Leader Positive Mood and Group Performance," *Journal of Applied Social Psychology* 25.9 (1995): 778-794.

20. Cf. Ornstein, 29.

21. Philip Watkins, "Gratitude and Subjective Well-Being," *The Psychology of Gratitude*, ed. Robert Emmons and Michael McCullough (New York: Oxford UP, 2004), 176.

22. Aristotle, *Ethica Nicomachea (Nicomachean Ethics)*, trans. W. Ross, in *Great Books of the Western World*, vol. 9, ed. Robert Hutchins (Encyclopedia Britannica, 1952), Book I, chapter 1 , 1103a14-26 (p. 348). I added emphasis to this quotation and also transliterated the Greek word for "ethos."

23. *Ibid.*, 103a34-1103b2 (pp. 348-349), emph. add.

24. Kandel (1976), 11.

25. Cf. Walter Freemans, *Societies of Brains: A Study in the Neuroscience of Love and Life* (Hillsdale, NJ: Lawrence Erlbaum, 1995); Daniel Stern, *The Interpersonal World of the Infant: A View from Psychoanalysis and Developmental Psychology* (New York: Basic, 1985), 40-41.

26. Kandel (1976), 540. Freeman writes that "[l]earning. . . requires that discrimination be attended by habituation, which may include atrophy of axonal and dendritic branches and the programmed death of whole neurons (apoptosis)" (Freeman [1995], 114).

27. Ornstein 30. For more on the phenomenon of noise, with a theological treatment, see: Christopher Rodkey, "Form, Fragmentation, and Theonomy: Noise as an Expression of Reality," M.Div. thesis, University of Chicago (Chicago, IL), 2002; a section of which was published as Christopher Rodkey, Reconsidering Noise in Theology and in Praxis," *Doxology* 21 (2004): 72-91. Also: Barbara Brown Taylor, *When God is Silent* (Cambridge, Mass.: Cowley, 1998), 31ff.

28. Ornstein, 31.

29. Pierre Bourdieu, *Outline of a Theory of Practice*, trans. Richard Nice (Cambridge, England: Cambridge UP, 1977), 78.

30. *Ibid.*, 80.

31. *Ibid.*, 82.

32. Russon, 46.

33. *Ibid.*, emph. add.

34. Russon, 46, "determinancy" is emphasized.

35. *Ibid.*, 46-47.

36. *Ibid.*, 47. Cf. Christopher Rodkey, Review of *Human Experience, Philosophical Practice* 2.1 (2006): 61-63.

37. Kandel (1976), 600; Ornstein, 130-131; Stern, 40-41.

38. Emmons, 9.

39. Cf. Freeman (1995), 114.

40. Cf. D. Brown 105.

41. d'Aquili and Newberg (1999), 26.

42. *Ibid.*, 89.

43. d'Aquili and Newberg: "a liturgical sequence that employs both aspects of arousal and of quiencence—some rapid songs, some slow hymns; some words of love; some words of fear; stories of glory, stories with morals; prayers exalting God and

prayers asking for help—will allow for the participants to experience religion in the most powerful way.... If a ritual has just the right rhythms, however, the participants may briefly experience something a step further. If the arousal and quiescent systems are activated during ritual, then they may experience a breakdown of the self-other dichotomy" (d'Aquili and Newberg [1999], 106). Gibson reports on the research on monastic lifestyles by the University of Chicago historian Rachel Fulton: "Within the haven of the monastery, they endeavored to transform each daily action into a devotional exercise, developing a rigorous, complex ritual of prayer that the written word could not encompass. 'Prayer is not entirely verbal,' Fulton says. 'Something is not simply a prayer by speaking of it.' Prayer also relies on belief, affective chant and posture, personal associations, and historical or scriptural allusions. 'It's not enough to read the book, you have to *be* the book. The monks I'm studying—most of them Benedictines... --'had a good understanding of the tension between what they know and what they did, between intellect and empathy,' Fulton says. 'They would sing a psalm, and it opened up this incredible world for them, a whole chain of resonances from what was happening the last time they sang it, or the beautiful painting they saw of the Virgin Mary, or from their monastic education'" (Gibson, 39). Cf. George Mandler, "Consciousness: Respectable, Useful, and Probably Necessary," *Essential Sources in the Scientific Study of Consciousness*, eds. Bernard Baurs, William Bowls, and James Newman (Cambridge, MA: MIT UP, 2003), 29; Ornstein, 120, 122.

44. Cf. Benzon, 189.

45. Freeman (1997), 70.

46. Cf. Kosfeld, et al, 673.

47. Benzon, 81-82. d'Aquili and Newberg: "Ritual is usually stereotyped or repetitive over time... [ritual] results in some greater coordination between individuals toward some common goal or purpose. Ritual behavior occurs in many animal species, including human beings, and it is critical to the development of behaviors of a social... nature. Thus, ritual might be performed by a group of people through song, dance, or the telling of stories. The telling of stories specific to a particular religious tradition forms its myth structure" (d'Aquili and Newberg [1999], 5).

48. Benzon, 81.

49. *Ibid.*, 189. For more on the role of oxytocin, social differentiation, and social individuation: Mahler, Pine, and Bergman, 52, 55ff.; Stern 241; and Allan Schore, *Affect Regulation and the Origin of the Self* (Hillside, NJ: Lawrence Erlbaum, 1994), 99-103, 112-113.

50. Bell, 79, 80; Bourdieu, 112.

51. Aidan Kavanaugh, *On Liturgical Theology* (Collegeville, MN: Liturgical, 1992), 88.

52. Cf. Bourdieu, 114.

Chapter Five
Worship as Religious Education

Worship can be understood as religious education within the neurological paradigm proposed by how our brains work and the philosophical notion of habituation. Habituation does not come naturally to us; rather, habituation is *enforced* upon us by culture, family, authority figures, and even our own desires. The question for this chapter, then, is *how can worship habituate religious experience?*

RELIGIOUS EDUCATION AS A REJECTION OF CHURCH

Going to church for many children, from their parents' perspective, is like herding unleashed cats through a boring museum. Sitting still and quiet; witnessing rituals that are rarely (or barely) explained; being tokenized, compartmentalized, and even *pedagogically abused* by children's sermons; singing songs older than their grandparents from hymnals their parents complain about as "not like the 'old one'"—it is no wonder why many children in traditional or mainline churches find the experience intolerable. I am being cynical, but I hope that my point is taken. If traditional church experience is going to be meaningful to the young, children must be positively *habituated* into the experience. We must remember that there are few places in children's and teens' lives where they encounter people of other ages and generations who are not related to them; there are far fewer places where they may be accepted without the masks and identities that the schoolyard and popular culture impose upon them. Teens especially live in a poisonous culture that *we adults* have manufactured; we should not be surprised when teens are reluctant to taste waters from a new fountain, even if it is a life- and self-affirming spring.

In 1994 two United Church of Christ pastors, Elizabeth Felts and Anthony Robinson, issued a document on the then-current state of religious education called *New Occasions Teach New Duties*. They recount a typical situation of religious education in mainline churches throughout the United States today:

> My local church had always conducted worship and Sunday school simultaneously, following a pattern of church life when the church was founded in the 1950s. From 10:00 to 11:00 every Sunday morning, the adults went to the sanctuary for worship, while the youth and children went to classrooms for Sunday school.
>
> For many folks, this was a convenient schedule. Weekly religious commitments could be fulfilled in sixty minutes' time. Parents of young children got to worship in peace while experienced teachers imparted the faith to their children. Children learned about being Christians through educational programs designed specifically for their age group. Adults could worship free from the distractions that restless children sometimes bring. These were all attractive reasons to keep the kids in one place and the adults in another.

The long-term effects, however, revealed problems with this model of religious education, noting, "[w]e were an age-segregated church." They explain, "[o]ur children were not getting regular, sustained opportunities to learn from the accumulated wisdom of our older adults and to challenge the prevailing cultural assumption that life and beauty end at retirement." But the effects reached further than just the children's experience.

> Our young parents [who taught Sunday school], many of whom were living far from their own parents, were not able to benefit from the "surrogate grandparenting" of the church's older adults. Our older adults, who often feel marginalized in a youth-oriented society, were further marginalized by worshiping in an "adults-only" sanctuary devoid of the energy and love of children.
>
> What is more, we were raising a generation of children who rarely got to experience worship in its fullness, who were uncomfortable and bored with it, and who would become a generation of adults who had no experience or understanding of worship and would likely abandon it. Because my realm of activity on Sunday mornings was in the sanctuary, I never got to know the names—let [alone] the interests and personalities—of our church's children.[1]

This is a familiar situation to my own professional church experience and surely many of my readers' church experiences. Clearly, the church sanctuary is identified by many church communities as an *adult* space, and the education wing is *kid* space.

One congregation that employed me as an educator exemplified everything about this model of religious education. Many years ago, the congregation and Sunday school had dwindled to the point where they eliminated the education hour before church, and had a small one- or two-room Sunday school that met during the church hour; children would leave worship after the Bible readings and before the sermon. When the population and demographics of the surrounding town shifted into the church's favor, and the number of elementary-aged children skyrocketed in the town, naturally, the Sunday school grew. As a response, by the time the children reached Jr. High School and began their confirmation classes, the confirmands were required to teach the classes to respond to the growth of the Sunday School program. After confirmation, youth were given more autonomy in teaching Sunday school classes, nearly always without adult supervision. There eventually were enough youth to have a separate Sr. High class, which was held during the church hour; *adult worship commenced without the teens.* Consequently, adult religious education dwindled to just a few faithful on a weeknight, and that small group eventually disbanded to meet only during the seasons of Advent and Lent. It is my understanding that similar situations and conditions occur in many other "mainline" Christian churches.

My observation of this church's situation (I arrived at the church around the peak of the Sunday school program) was one of *shock*. The education wing had become a "kid space," as mentioned before, to the point that the teens were more or less running the Sunday School. During school breaks and big events at the high school (dances, homecoming games, musicals, etc.) the Sunday School would have "Family Sundays," an attempt at a *pan-generational* worship experience,* but the reality was that parents, youth, and children would not come to church on Family Sundays. When the staff inquired of some parents, they found that parents did not want to deal with their kids in church: it was too much of a hassle, they didn't want to "ruin church" for their kids (that is, by making them come to church); the teens simply refused to come to church when there was no Sunday School; or parents even explicitly stated that *Sunday worship is not for teenagers.* We had not only *habituated* children and teenagers into leaving church when they came to church, we had *habituated* the adults into identifying Sunday worship as "adult space" for "adults only." Again, I understand that this is not an uncommon situation happening in many churches in the United States today.

At the first youth retreat that I led, just a few months into my tenure as the youth pastor at this church, I celebrated communion with the teens, and I was taken aback by the fact that even the most active youth who came to church every Sunday had *no idea* what it was we were doing together. They had only experienced the Eucharist a couple of times, and they simply had no idea what to *do*, how to behave, or even have more than peripheral understanding of one of the most basic rituals of the Christian faith. In other words, they did not have a

---

* By a "pan-generational worship experience" I mean a truly representative worship experience that acknowledges *all* generations, and not just *some*. (For example, the catch-phrase *inter-generational worship* often simply refers to an adult worship service that makes *accommodations* for children or youth. *Multi-generational* could just refer to one or two generations—such as Baby Boomers and their children.)

group of people around them to copy or *mimic* the motions of the ritual while at the youth retreat. Clearly, these teens had not been adequately habituated into the worship life of the church. I even noticed that college students, when occasionally visiting the church while on school breaks, also left with the procession of children and youth during worship out to Sunday School, to "hang out" as *emeritus* members of the Sr. High class, to assist family members who were teaching Sunday school, or to socialize with the sexton or the Children's minister.

Again, we had *taught* a significant population of the church to *not* go to church when *going* to church. The church had created a *habitus* of church experience to the children and teens that involved *separating themselves* from the other generations while present at church. Religious educational theorist James White writes that many congregations, like mine and many

> [o]thers seemingly train young people—almost systematically—*not* to worship, *not* to learn in and from sacred services, *not* to break bread with people of different ages. Many duly dedicated infants grow up with little familiarity with their born-into faith community's sacred practices. This can easily happen when the hour for religious education is the same as that of the worship service. "Convenience scheduling" to "do church in sixty minutes" presents students—as well as teachers—from attending worship. A teenager may have a Sunday School Perfect Attendance Pin with year bars dangling down to the belt and yet know nothing about liturgical life.[2]

White adds, I suspect somewhat hyperbolically, "[i]t is reported that some graduate theological seminaries have to do remedial 'Basic Worship' courses to prepare divinity students for the worship work of parish ministry!"[3] Clearly, worshiping disciples "must be *made*," habituated into worshiping habits and practices over time.[4]

THE SYNAPTIC GOSPEL

The *good news* of this study is that a neurological paradigm for thinking about worship offers a renewed vision for the possibility of communal formation and individual discipleship and liberation. I believe it is obvious that religious education programs are essential for a sustained religious community's mission of proclaiming Jesus to, and developing moral character within, the young. But pan-generational experience, given its rarity in our current situation, is also educational to both children and adults. The very presence of all generations—infants, children, "tweens," teenagers, young adults, quarter-lifers, young parents and mid-life singles, "empty nesters," pre-retirement, post-retirement, and those at the end of life—joining in the sharing of common stories, singing songs, praying and worshiping together *is religious education for all who are involved.*[5]

The openness of the life-cycle in religious communities, when expressly asserted by the presence of the varieties and manifestations of the life-cycle, is not only a *subversive* cultural activity but is a witness to the endurance and sustainability of a shared faith. We live in an American culture that is mythically obsessed with individualism and a society that simultaneously rewards empty homogenization, apathy, and complacency. Jill Fraser offers this American story in her book, *White Collar Sweatshop*:

> Another source of mine told me about his friend Ron, who had spent his career working up the ladder at Goodyear. "His department at one time had two hundred or so people in it. Now it's down to fourteen. The ones who are left— they don't make waves." My source paused, then added, "You can sense it everywhere. They don't say too much. But when people open up to you, you realize they don't care how they do their jobs. These are people who built these companies. They're going out feeling like losers. It's been very damaging."[6]

The above story is not uncommon among many people sitting in our church pews, and even more who are not on our membership rolls. Clearly, an *interruption* of life being lived unreflectively and in such a *spiritually-incarcerated* state is sorely needed. To remain relevant and prophetic, Christian worship must be reclaimed as an inherently *subversive* activity. Against the poisonous culture, the church must become a *circle of empathy*, care, support, and love. As an essential component of religious education, worship also provides a forum for storytelling, liberation, and self-actualization.[7] This does not simply happen automatically in most religious communities, as there are boundaries to the communities and, left to our own devices, we would often rather go it alone than admit our finitude and difficulty in leading life's journey on our own.

The *good news* is, however, that we can habituate ourselves into religious communities, and our biological mechanisms are wired such that genuine, empathic *community is possible*. Walter Freeman writes that "[n]eural mechanisms by which solipsistic knowledge can be created, made public, and validated between individuals become clear only in the context of intentional action," meaning that we extend our individuated realities to others' presence and realities *intentionally*, on purpose, or through some kind of habituation. "This problem lies not in translating or mapping knowledge from one brain onto another," Freeman continues, "but rather in establishing mutual understanding and trust through shared actions during which brains create the channels [and] codes" which "proceed [through] reciprocal mappings of information in dialogues." Just *talking* or communicating *is not enough*: community must take on symbols or myths to be deeply ingrained into the individuals' lives. To make an analogy, Freeman adds, "[i]t takes more than a telephone line...to make a call to a foreign country."[8] The social apparatus needed is a group or *ecclesia*; the stories are provided by the scriptures with the living human documents of the individuals; and the rituals develop from *both* the handed-down traditions *and* new traditions that naturally arise out of the group.[9]

HABITUATION AS DISCIPLESHIP

The *good news* is also that we may have a renewed thinking of individual liberation within our neurological paradigm. If worship provides the space where our brains can become syncopated with one another to be open to shared emotions and empathy, though the stories of others we gain self-knowledge and learn to self-actualize. To do this, Edith Stein taught, requires "a transparency to one's own emotions" and the ability to "read" others' emotions as a means of "reading" one's own; in fact, one might even argue (as have Robert Roberts and W. Wood) that the ability to read and appreciate one's own emotions is an emotional mode in itself.[10]

Storytelling, as I have been mentioning occasionally, is one of the primary ways by which we empathically and neurologically open ourselves to others.[11] Protestant Christian worship nearly always centers its experience around the reading of the "Word" or Bible, or the telling of stories in sermons. Eastern Orthodoxy (as well as several significant strands of Western esotericism, such as Freemasonry) has a long and rich history of locating story through the dramatic and visual liturgical arts. The emphasis on storytelling in Catholic worship places significant emphasis upon the re-membering of Christ's suffering through the sacramental ritual of the Eucharist.[12] Many liturgical acts assume or re-enact primordial stories or stories representing a masking of a taboo or shared cultural memory of social norms.[13]

The rite—or in some traditions, the sacrament—of confirmation has a confirmand, usually a teenager, re-enacting her infant baptism. The whole point of confirmation as a re-enactment of baptism resides in the fact that the act of baptism itself is usually *absent* from the rite, that is, it re-enacts the baptism *without parents or guardians immediately present.* The confirmation rite at once enforces the confirmand to ritualistically live in her own story and, for the adults who were present at the initial baptism, recall the confirmands' and their own baptisms.[14] Beyond this, confirmation offers the opportunity to the confirmand and the individuals in the community to negotiate their own identities around the event, to "reimagine our memories" of our own and others' baptisms, confirmations, and "signposts" of the life cycle.[15] The mistake often made by religious communities around the rite of confirmation is to liturgically or communally treat the act of confirmation as a "destination" rather than a signpost. Such thinking sends the message to the confirmand that the spiritual change enacted in herself in the rite of confirmation is a *graduation*, rather than an *affirmation* of one significant step—one among many others—on the journey of the life cycle. Regardless, whenever memories are re-imagined or recast ritualistically the "potential for change exists" for the performing, witnessing, or receiving the ritual.[16]

THINKING AND LIVING LITURGICALLY

As such, storytelling can be a primary means of grafting one's own biography onto the Biblical or liturgical narrative that is shared in community.[17] The language, stories, symbols, allusions, metaphors, vocal inflections, and eventually, the liturgical space which shape the storytelling-voices *themselves* may serve as neurological triggers. These triggers re-call a *midrash* of our own selves into the Bible passage, testimony, sermon, missional or stewardship appeal, or liturgical action enacted in worship.[18]

One should recall that the Christian Sabbath, observed by most Christian communities on Sunday, is a recalling of the regeneration of Easter, even on Sundays that are liturgically differentiated from Easter—such as the first Sundays of Advent, Christmastide, or Epiphany; Pentecost, or in some traditions, "Kingdomtide"; as well as other special days like Mother's and Father's Day, and Sundays related to civic holidays, such as Memorial Day. The Sunday gathering is itself a re-calling of resurrection, which is inherently a symbol of the transition from the tomb and Hell to new life, a further incarnation of Spirit into flesh in the Risen Christ, or the justice of God in a messianic defeat of evil. Beyond this, the very gathering of Christians on the Sabbath is also indicative of a remembrance of the primordial divine act of creation—that is, that God rested at the end of first week of creation. This is to say that Sabbath-gathering is a renewal: a starting-over, a *tehomic* uplifting over the chaotic week, an opportunity to be refreshed and liberated from the poisons that await outside of the sanctuary. The symbols are rich and varied, contributing to its depth of significance. Sabbath-gathering is regenerative, liberative, resurrecting, and life-affirming.[19]

By living and re-living, telling and re-calling, discovering and re-casting, acting out and praying the stories that we share in community, we learn to not only *think Biblically*, as philosopher Paul Ricoeur suggests, but we habituate ourselves into *thinking* and *living liturgically*.[20] Living liturgically is a kind of discipleship that is transformative and liberative. For the liturgical actor, life is re-created by ritualizing one's own reality, being open to new habituations, and intermingling one's own habituation to coinciding realities with other individuals..[21] The challenge of others' habituations to our owns challenges and strengthens our habituative plasticity. Thinking and living liturgically opens the possibility for our imaginations, stories, and symbols to be newly regenerated and anchored, and to have a multiplicity of anchorings within the hexity and ever-expanding matrices of our constructed realities.[22] Liturgical living is individually and communally *transformative*; to live and think liturgically requires a constant and perpetual exchange of meaning-construction into our past, present, and our futures.[23] To live liturgically is to live universally and communally, it acknowledges that no matter what, when "you go on a solitary walk, you take other people with you."[24]

Living liturgically is like living *ludologically*, living the "game of life" with an expanded board. The rules, restrictions on strategies, and limitations on game participants are broken down and no longer restrictive. The game provides a completely different "mental dress" to life than previously thought possible—for example, one obviously plays chess with a different initial gaming disposition than poker.[25] Rituals often create parameters for the religious experience, but one who lives liturgically may move from church to church, from ritual set to set, and from home to work to find meaningful religious ritual in all contexts.[26] The games' rules and participants may change occasionally, but to live liturgically is to rise above "objectives," "winners," and "losers": it is to live for an *autotelic* enjoyment of life itself and all of those who are encountered along the journey.[27] *It is, in essence, to live—to habituate in—the Kingdom of God.*

CONCLUSION:
THE NEED FOR NEW RITUAL

The *synaptic gospel*—that our religious "experience and biology are constant companions"—is not only good news, but is an *evangelistic* call to serve the humanity with which we find universality.[28] David Hogue writes that

> [i]n pastoral care, we often encounter stories that have no rituals—no ways to mark or acknowledge life's changes—no ways to bring people into new ways of being and living. Losses like divorce, sending a child off to college, or the death of a child can bring suffering into our lives in ways that defy words. Too often, suffering persons have no opportunities to ritualize these experiences.[29]

While some religious traditions do have defined rituals for some of these life events, many do not; regardless, Hogue's point is clear. New rituals are needed for contemporary humanity. For those who live liturgically, new rituals naturally become a part of our day-to-day experience, but in service to others we can include others in our rituals—whether they realize it or not—or create ritual experiences for others.[30]

To live liturgically is to live honestly and positively. This is not to say that we live in a saccharine world, but rather we live in the Paschal desire for the New Creation which is rising up and about from our Christian community.[31] A significant affirmation of this Christian hope may be attributed to the reality that our brains physiologically demonstrate that we may rise above the banality of complacent existence to affirm a self-actualization for ourselves and ritualize the possibility of habituating into sustaining communities. And, with the grace of God, living this Kingdom of God will lead us into a final and ultimate joy.

Notes: Chapter Five

1. Elizabeth Felts and Anthony Robinson, *New Occasions Teach New Duties: A Renewed Vision of the Teaching Church* (Cleveland, OH: UCC Division of Education Publication, 1994), 46-47. The authors continue: "The one-hour schedule was, in many ways, well suited to the realities of life in the 1990s. Our families are overprogrammed and accustomed to compressing many activities into as little time as possible. Busy families often take the 'divide-and-conquer' approach to family tasks, and so they are comfortable with a Sunday morning schedule that allows them to accomplish everything in one hour: children learn, adults pray, everyone gets a little something" (Felts and Robinson, 48).

2. James White, *Intergenerational Religious Education* (Birmingham, AL: Religious Education Press, 1988), 46-47.

3. *Ibid.*, 47, citing Arlo Duba, "Seminarians Who Have Never Been To Church," *Monday Morning* (3 Dec. 1979), 10-11.

4. Felts and Robinson, 49; cf. Csikszentmihalyi, 67-68.

5. Cf. Robert Fuller, *Religion & the Life Cycle* (Philadelphia: Fortress, 1988), 53ff.

6. Jill Fraser, *White-Collar Sweatshop* (New York: Norton, 2001), 111-112.

7. Abraham Maslow, *The Farther Reaches of Human Nature* (New York: Viking, 1971), 169.

8. Freeman (2000), 415; cf. Fred Hanna, "Community Feeling, Empathy, and Intersubjectivity: A Phenomenological Framework," *Individual Psychology* 53.1 (1996), 23. Freeman continues: "Therefore, to say that a brain is solipsistic is to say that it grows like a neuron within itself, and that it has a boundary around itself in much the way that a neuron has a boundary membrane entirely around itself, preserving its unity and integrity. The barrier is not merely the skin and bone around each brain" (Freeman [2000], 415).

9. Csikszentmihalyi writes: "[t]he audiences at today's live [music] performances, such as rock concerts, continue to partake in...ritual elements; there are few other occasions which large numbers of people witness the same event together, think and feel the same things, and process the same information" (Csikszentmihalyi, 110).

10. Roberts and Wood, 18.

11. Cf. Judith Plaskow, "The Coming of Lilith: Toward a Feminist Theology," *Womanspirit Rising: A Feminist Reader in Religion*, eds. Carol Christ and Judith Plaskow, 1992 ed. (New York: Harper San Francisco, 1992), esp. 200ff.; Edward Wimberly, *Recalling Our Own Stories* (San Francisco: Jossey-Bass, 1997).

12. Cf, Christopher Rowland, "Eucharist as Liberation from the Present," *The Sense of the Sacramental*, ed. David Brown and Ann Loades (Sewanee, TN: SPCK, 1995), 214.

13. See, for example, George Bataille, *Erotism*, trans. Mary Dalwood (San Francisco: City Lights, 1975), esp. 40-54; and Daly, 110ff.

14. Cf. Hogue, 100.

15. McAdams and Bauer, 90; Hogue, 158, 130.

16. Hogue, 158.

17. Cf. Baruch Urieli, *Male and Female: Developing Human Empathy* (London: Temple Lodge, 2001), 65-66.

18. Cf. Panksepp (1998), 309.

19. Cf. Paulo Freire, *The Politics of Education: Culture, Power, and Liberation*, trans. Donaldo Macedo (New York: Bergin & Garvey, 1985), 123.

20. Paul Ricoeur and André LaCocque, *Thinking Biblically*, trans. David Pellauer (Chicago: U Chicago P, 1998); and Paul Ricoeur, "The Question of Proof in Freud's

Psychoanalytic Writings," *Journal of the American Psychoanalytic Association* 25 (1977): 835-871; Stern 15.

21. Cf. Felts and Robinson, 50ff.; B. Keith Rowe, "The Renewal of Baptism/Initiation," *Doxology* 4 (1987), 27.

22. Cf. Hogue, 160.

23. Naomi Goldenberg, *Changing of the Gods: Feminism & the End of Traditional Religions* (Boston: Beacon, 1979), 101.

24. Jean Decety, quoted in Gibson, 39.

25. David Sally, "Dressing the Mind Properly for the Game," *The Neuroscience of Social Interaction*, eds. Christopher Frith and Daniel Wolpert (Oxford, England: Oxford UP, 2004), 284.

26. Cf. *ibid.*, 288ff.

27. Cf. Csikszentmihalyi, 87-69; James Brown, "Faith, Flesh, and Feeling," *Worship* 60.3 (2001): 227.

28. Hogue 158; cf. Rick Warren, *The Purpose-Driven Church* (Grand Rapids, MI: Zondervan, 1995), 252ff.

29. Hogue, 121.

30. The need may also be, parenthetically, to disassemble older rituals, or rituals whose relevance has eclipsed or whose outward symbols may no longer be spiritually or politically worthwhile—see, for example, my article, "A Polemic Against the 'Festival of the Christian Home,'" in *Sacramental Life* 17.2 (2005): 18-23. Feminist spiritual writers have written on this need for new liturgy also; see essays by Nelle Morton, Judith Plaskow, Aviva Cantor, Penelope Washbourn, Starhawk, Zauzsanna Budapest in the excellent volume *Womanspirit Rising*, eds. Carol Christ and Judith Plaskow, 1992 ed. (New York: Harper San Francisco, 1992). I cannot underestimate the gravity that these writings have influenced the directions of my thinking here.

31. Cf. George, 778-794.

Chapter Six
An Ecology of Liturgy:
Habituating Liturgically with Youth

We may take these patterns of new thinking into numerous directions: further research; response to new science; re-thinking from fresh, new philosophical perspectives; and, hopefully, *better ministries*. The most practical and obvious suggestions are to invent and find new ways to engage the body in worship and ritual at all stages of the life cycle. Drumming, for example, is becoming more common as a spiritual practice in progressive churches—both in small groups and in pan-generational worship.[1] Employing physical movement through the outdoor stations of the cross; reclaiming the Catholic tradition of perfuming the sanctuary; learning and repeating ancient creeds, prayers, scriptures, and even catechisms to memory all emerge, under our neurological paradigm, as legitimate and appropriate ways to habituate people of all ages through an *ecology* of liturgical living.[2]

The greatest challenge before all churches, if not all religious communities in our current state of secularization and secularizing, is to teach young people *what worship is*. To do this, we must also teach what worship *means* and *how it works*. For worship to be truly life-changing, the end of religious education must be to teach liturgical living. In practice, however, as we have learned, living liturgically does not happen automatically; rather, it is a *habituated,* long-haul process that enforces the unraveling of conformity to the poisonous world. Children's and youth ministries must provide an *ecology*—an environment, an *oasis*—for opportunities to live liturgically, to evolve new habituations, and to breathe for air in a world of poisonous, drowning waters.[3]

Principlism

A great deal of ink has been spilled over defining best practices for youth ministry; what the new trends or new fads are to "hook" in teens. My experience in youth ministry is that while these resources are hit or miss, it is much more helpful to understand and know the community in which one ministers, and work within those contexts, and offer sustenance where one is able. I am unconvinced that there is a youth ministry "model" that answers the needs of a single youth group—the respected youth ministry theorist Mark DeVries has identified no less than *nineteen* models of youth ministry![4] A neurologically-informed paradigm of youth ministry acts upon *principles,* rather than *programmatic models.* Principles identified from our journey may include *empathy, pan-generational experience, habituation, thinking liturgically,* and *living liturgically.* Further principles may be determined by an individual community's "local theology."[5] As a ministry of a larger, pan-generational circle of worshipers, youth ministry should offer an ecology of opportunities for any or all of these kinds of activities.

As a "principlism," I mean to emphatically reiterate that there is not one solution, not one liturgy or liturgical style, not one program that will work in all communities; rather, a *paradigm* based upon *principles* is a more useful methodology for localized ministerial practice. I take the term principlism from the philosophical discipline of biomedical ethics, where the idea is primarily attributed to philosophical ethicists Tom Beauchamp and James Childress and their highly influential book, *Principles of Biomedical Ethics.*[6] Simply stated, for Beauchamp and Childress, medical practice operates within an environment which includes varying community-based standards of ethics; the personal values of patients, and practitioners, medical administrators, and patients' families; varying balances of values and evidences for moral action, and so on. Because of these competing ethical systems in practice, Beauchamp and Childress propose four *principles* of medical ethics: respect for autonomy, nonmaleficience (that is, the Hippocratic dictum of "do no harm"), beneficence ("do good"), and justice.

Certainly, there are problems with principlism, especially regarding what happens when one must do harm to do good? Or what does one do when there are conflicting definitions of "doing good" (or "doing harm")?[7] Principlism primarily works *when there is agreement in a community about shared values.* Given the public nature of medical practice, the problems surrounding the application of principlism with medical ethics situations are that doctors usually do not only treat patients with the same values. Furthermore, values are often dictated from non-medical sources—lawyers and politicians. The *good news* for ministry is that in small groups we can define shared values more easily, even if the values will never be absolutely uniform. *Different communities will obviously have different values, but the different communities together may agree on certain principles that connect them.* This is my point for importing a philosophical "principlism" for the theoretical framework of pastoral practice.

For example, I once participated in a youth ministry conference session on baptism and confirmation where the debate was whether baptism should be offered without *catechesis,* that is, whether a teenager should be baptized freely without a preparatory phase or "baptism class." In other words: is the sacrament of baptism an *invitation* to faith or a *public sign* of faith? The group's discussion went into the history of Christian initiation and confirmation, as well as the scriptural account of Philip's baptism of the Ethiopian eunuch as the first Gentile Christian (Acts 8:26-40). I suggested to the group that my congregation at the time actually did not require baptism for confirmation or church membership—a notion that evoked laughter from the group! For the others, I argued, a required public baptism is a restoration of everyone else's baptism, and allows for empathy within a community at the act of confirmation, when several people reflect upon the baptism and childhood of the confirmand. The sacrament then provides a framework for pan-generational worship.

I am proposing that through a principle-based approach to pan-generational ministry, confirmation is not just a liturgical action where a teenager is the subject of the church conferring a rite, but is a *participatory process* involving church members from every spectrum of the life cycle. Beyond this, requiring a ritual that is not meaningful to teens robs them of possibility becoming legitimate religious thinkers in the community, let alone desiring baptism or participation later in life. The local values of my congregation were obviously quite different from the others, but I believe that contradictory practices—such as requiring baptism for confirmation—can be equally meaningful, theory-laden, and authentic in different communities following the same principles. My point is the following: pastoral practice is more meaningful within local contexts when the practice follows commonly-known principles, as opposed to a deontologically- or polity-imposed theology or theoretical meta-narrative.

TEACHING LITURGICAL ECOLOGY[*]

Teaching liturgy can occur at many different times in a youth program; teaching takes many different forms—didactic, service-oriented, activity-based, talk-based, musical, dramatic, family-oriented, and gender-specific forms, to name a few—and the teaching of liturgy can be rather *sneaky*. I have found retreats, for example, to be a good context for teaching liturgy. I have designed retreats or overnights around the practice of saint calendars, the writing of creeds, covenantal understandings of the Eucharist, and even writing calls to worship for special liturgical observations using *The Common Book of Prayer*.[8] On retreats, we follow the daily office (cycles of prayer throughout the day) of a Protestant secular order.[9] A key element of lock-ins for youth might include midnight Eucharist by candlelight. Similarly, reflective time during service trips with youth always include communion and explicit conversations about the

---

[*] I wish to draw attention to the notes to this chapter, which contain not only my references but also many resources that I have found helpful and highly recommend.

connection between social justice and sacramental theology.[10] Confirmands' parents present a Bible to the youth in worship to begin their confirmation classes; the confirmands' feet are later washed at the end of their two-year class cycle.[11] In addition to rehearsing together the Christian liturgical calendar, our confirmands also learn basics about the religious calendars, especially the festivals and observances of Judaism, which for the youth culminates in an observance of Yom HaShoah.[12]

Other methods of teaching liturgy are less explicit or obvious, but are subtle essentials in contributing to an ecology of habituating liturgy. Following my example of using the Jewish calendar, for Purim, we read the book of Esther together—using the Purim gragger (*ra'ashan*), a noisemaker, or drums and cymbals at every mention of the name of *Haman*—during a night of raucousness and games.[13] When youth eat together, bread and grapes are on the table and we call our meals "love feasts." We reaffirm our baptisms in prayer by sprinkling water on each other when sitting on the floor in circles.[14] We journal together as part of small-group worship.[15] Our sexuality education group begins each class session with a formal chalice lighting.[16] Some older youth discuss the *I Ching* or the symbols of Tarot cards to make sense of the ways in which symbols construct reality.[17] Occasional book or covenant groups around teenage spirituality written by teens—such as Margorie Corbman's *A Tiny Step Away from Deepest Faith*—help teens liturgize and find symbols from their past and graft them onto their own spiritual autobiographies.[18] Children's sermons, vespers breaks on nature hikes, or church-related Scouting events are good opportunities to connect stories from the great world religions, especially from the Native American traditions, to life lessons.[19] I have arranged for posters to be made of a church's stained glass for teens to display a piece of the church building in their college dormitory. In all of these activities, it is important for teens to be individually creative and expressive, and for the group to acknowledge the individual's experience and meaning-making, and to communally enter each other's self-expression and self-actualizing projections.[20]

The local community may place heavier emphasis on certain holidays and rituals than others. The only Protestant church that I have ever participated in an Ascension Day worship (as separate from Ascension Sunday!) was one with prominent stained glass windows depicting the ascension of Christ. September 11th had a very different significance in a church that I served that was in the midwestern United States than another church that I served, who lost a beloved Sunday School teacher in the collapse of the World Trade Center. Baptism and confirmation have different relevancies in different congregations; many wonderful congregations only celebrate communion a few times per year. The intentional *absence* of some liturgical traditions within communities might mean more than what is practiced; the radical silence of the Quaker tradition is certainly indicative of this, as is the nearly four hundred year ban on the sacrament of communion in the Schwenkfelder Church (a small denomination with roots in the Radical Reformation)![21]

With teenagers, it is easy to construct meaningful worship experiences and celebrations around holidays that they invent. Use their sense of humor. Recall, for example, the cultural phenomenon that responded to the television episode of *Seinfeld* that introduced the winter holiday Festivus. As it happens, Festivus was introduced to *Seinfeld* writer Dan O'Keefe by his father, Daniel O'Keefe, Sr., partially out of a familial need for a secular holiday that was not commercialized or overtly political. Festivus, "a festival for the rest of us," was one of many holidays and family rituals invented and practiced in the O'Keefe household, which included "unbirthdays," family election day, and the "Polish hour."[22] Teens can develop special worship experiences around school breaks, finals and mid-terms, proms, graduations, family events, or other community activities. The scriptures are inexhaustibly ripe with appropriate readings for even the smallest life changes to our young people—I have found that the book of Lamentations, for example, is effective when emphatically read with youth and college students—so that rituals, discussions and other "events" may be tailored for the situation.[23]

A liturgical ecology does not only include learning about liturgy. Service projects and social justice can teach empathy and lead youth to be more empathic during their local worship service—within their own circles of empathy. Participation in pan-generational activities, like women's or specialized interest groups within church communities, teach empathy and community. Musical and drama activities foster friendships and help youth self-actualize themselves in artistic ways. Youth leaders and ministers who live liturgically provide role modeling and serve as resource persons for discipleship, pastoral care, and one-on-one empathy. Clergy and youth workers can encourage parents to take the role of spiritual mentor and model for their children and youth.[24] If neurologically-informed youth ministries provide an ecology of, or an oasis of opportunities for, liturgical living, we provide a greater possibility for the habituations that foster a long-term, adult faith for young people.[25]

A CANDLELIGHT RITUAL
FOR ALL SAINTS' SUNDAY

The following is a ritual for All Saints' Sunday that I designed for a small church that had congregants from every age group. The goals were to engage the principles that I mentioned before: *empathy, pan-generational experience, habituation, thinking liturgically*, and *living liturgically*. The local values of the congregation suggested to me that All Saint's Sunday was very important to this congregation because of the large number of elderly members and the congregation's expectation that the pastor officiate many funerals outside of the church in the community—to the point that many congregants would come to funerals of people they did not know if their pastor was the officiant. As such, I invited every family member from the church's records of the deceased whose funerals performed by clergy from the church. Before I go into the ritual's detail, I wish to mention that before the ritual, I carefully explained exactly what was going to happen to the congregation during the sermon.

At the front of the sanctuary, before worship began, I placed about 150 unlit candles, so that everywhere one looked, candles were present. After the sermon and offering in the liturgy, the electric lights were dimmed and the names of all in the community who had passed away—church members, non-members, former members living far away, friends of members whose names were requested in advance—in the last twelve months were read. As each name is stated, a bell was tolled and a candle was lit.

Then the congregation began to sing the Taizé chant, "Jesus, Remember Me," repeatedly as I, as the pastor, escorted groups or families or groups of two to five persons forward to the candle area.[26] Once an individual or a group was standing before the montage of candles, each congregant was invited to say a name or a prayer for any loved one who has passed away and to light as many candles as they wish. In a few instances, extended moments of pastoral care were extended by me to some individuals, as well as grandparents reminding their grandchildren the names of deceased relatives whom the children had never met. All of this was very moving for the congregation to witness. Before the worship service, I also made sure to have a tray or two of candles ready for disabled or handicapped persons.

Following this ritual, after everyone who wanted had come forward, and the Taizé chant naturally ended, I poured water into the font—placed in a dignified manner near the entrance of the sanctuary—from a pitcher and blessed the water using the words typical of a baptism ritual. I then said a few words reminding the congregation of the significance of baptism in our shared beliefs regarding Christian death, as this congregation has a strong local baptismal theology. I concluded with a benediction that I took from Karl Rahner, which was printed in the church bulletin:

> It is said that You will come again, and this is true. But the word *again* is misleading. It won't really be "another" coming, because You have never really gone away. In the human existence which You made Your own for all eternity, You have never left us.
> . . . .
> Behold, You come. And Your coming is neither past nor future, but the present, which has only to reach its fulfillment. . . .
>
> O God who is to come, grant me the grace to live now, in the hour of your Advent, in such a way that I may merit to live in You forever, in the blissful hour of Your Eternity. *Amen.*[27]

This prayer was used throughout the weeks leading up to All Saint's Sunday, which, in my situation, involved a series of Sunday sermons on the theme of Second Coming, to intentionally lead into the themes of All Saint's Sunday and into the season of Advent.

I explained to the congregation that following the benediction that they may meditate or remain in silence with the candles and be mindful that when they turn their backs on the candles to leave the sanctuary, that they remain faithful that the candles all remain lit while they are not physically tending the flames, in the same manner of faith which we have in the promise of Eternal Life. While greeting people upon their exit, I directly invited them to touch the waters of the baptismal font.

This worship experience was deliberately designed to assert an affective approach to a special day on the liturgical calendar that had direct existential relevance to the worship participant. If anything, I attempted to give an overload of symbols regarding Christian death to deliver the importance and centrality of death to lived Christian experience: namely, to remind ourselves that death is not the *absence of being* but the *fulfillment of being*, that is to say, the *fulfillment of the promises* of Christian belief and baptism.[28] To me, the salient element in the ritual is defining the significance of leaving the sanctuary as a symbol of personal commitment to the Christian faith; since the one thing everyone must do as both individuals and a congregation is depart from the sanctuary. With tears of mourning or even a stare of ambivalence, each person must decide to leave: and one could not leave without noticing the candles and the events that had just transpired.

Hopefully, after witnessing the empathy with which the pastor expresses to the grieving before the candles, as well as the empathy between parent and child, the congregation will reflect God's empathy with each other upon departure. Teens experienced others' emotions, especially the emotions of those they might only marginally know within the church. The pan-generational congregation was teaching each other empathic ways of being; the liturgical space provided the means. The repetition of the Taizé chant created a contemplative, pan-generational rhythmic space that eventually, naturally ended. This worship experience might not work in every congregation, but it worked in this one. I encourage my readers to try new things, be creative, listen to the local theologies, be guided by the local values and shared principles. At bottom is a belief that actions change the actors, and over time, new rituals may change our ritualized habituations of the world.[29]

THINKING LITURGICALLY:
THE FESTIVAL OF THE CHRISTIAN HOME

The *liberative* change of the actor in the worship setting is our primary task; theological reflection is secondary, though theological reflection is necessary to habituate an individual into a liturgical ecology. I'll provide an example of a time when I saw signs of this with a teenage congregant.

Within some mainline Protestant denominations, both Mother's Day and the Festival of the Christian Home fall on the same Sunday every year, the second Sunday in May.[30] Many congregations have adopted the use of the "Festival of the Christian Home" as an alternative to Mother's Day because of, among other reasons, the painfulness of Mother's Day for some and as an acknowledgement that not every family necessarily has mothers. My first experience with "Festival of the Christian Home" came in one of my first ministerial positions; prior to this time, I had never heard of the Festival. The Festival was liturgically celebrated by this congregation because of the large number of single parents and unmarried couples in the church. The church staff, particularly the Senior Pastor, clearly felt that the replacement of Mother's Day with the Festival was politically correct and prided the congregation's celebration of the Festival as a matter of social justice. The Festival was, for this church and its staff, a formative piece of the identity of this congregation.

My immediate response to the Senior Pastor was: "Don't you think women might find it offensive that the celebration of the *home* is coincidentally also Mother's Day? You know, the whole 'women-should-be-in-the-home' thing?'" The senior pastor knit his eyebrows, and said *"Naaahh!,"* dismissing my concerns as total rubbish. As the new guy on the block, I kept my mouth shut, and moved on.

A few year's later, in a different congregation, the new Senior Pastor wanted to stress the Festival of the Christian Home instead of Mother's Day; and many on the ministerial staff had never heard of the Festival before. The Festival was obviously new to the congregation, as well. The Senior Pastor felt that the Festival was necessary as an act of justice and solidarity to single mothers and women without children. The worship service was awkward, and from my point of view, not particularly meaningful to the congregation; clearly, these concerns did not arise out of the local theological contexts, and Mother's Day is probably not the best time to announce a redefining of Mother's Day.

Immediately after the Festival service, however, one observant male youth member of the congregation made a particularly pointed observation, asking me sarcastically over e-mail, "Why don't we just coincidentally rename Father's Day 'Labor Day?'"

In his snarkiness, this teen made the connection of the disconnection between this liturgical observation and *essentialistic* conceptions of gender. Any argument to keep these two observances liturgically fused makes a philosophically reductionistic claim regarding gender difference aside from the fact that it seems that the Festival is designed to primarily be little more than a "re-labeling" to avoid some confrontations regarding Mother's Day.[31] The teen might not be able to articulate his sneering comment on a theoretical level, but the comment demonstrates good liturgical sensitivity. While there are religious communities where the Festival of the Christian Home might have deep meaning within their local theological contexts; from my perspective, this story indicates that for this teenage boy there are beginning signs of a social, political, and gendered reflection on the connection between community ritual and everyday living.[32]

THE CHILDREN'S SERMON AS LITURGICAL MOVEMENT

Shortly after the call to my current congregation, we had an interesting book study that engaged the contemporary challenges of mainline Protestant churches. These discussions were enormously helpful for me to culturally and theologically contextualize where exactly this congregation located themselves and to envision with them where and how to progress into the future. One project that I suggested to the group was to think about something old in the church that they could celebrate and make new. We talked a little bit about the *Heidelberg Catechism* and how we were renewing our use of it in the life of the church, but someone discovered that the current year was in fact the 75th anniversary of the wood and copper font in the church.

We talked a bit in our group about what the meaning of the font is, what it meant to the remnants of the Ladies' Aid Society who had commissioned it, and what baptism means for us in the church—yet the font was often hidden from view. In fact, when I first arrived as the pastor I asked where the font was and it was hidden in a corner near the women's restroom, outside of the sanctuary. We decided that before the year was over, we should have a celebration of the font with a worship of baptismal rededication. The lectionary often leans toward John the Baptist during Advent, so it was an appropriate time of year to renew our baptism by celebrating the font. The font was moved back into the sanctuary and placed in a more permanent and visible location, where I intended it to stay, and the congregation reclaimed the font as a central element of the worship space, rather than an inconvenient piece of furniture.

Consequently, following Christmas the final phase of the congregation's building project was about to commence, and everything that was not nailed down in the sanctuary had to be taken out, since the worship space was getting new walls and a few other upgrades. Our worship space for six weeks was going to be our new narthex, and we decided to have circular seating and to have the font be the central focus of the interim worship space. Our children's sermon on our final Sunday in the "old" sanctuary focused upon what are essential and inessential to the Christian faith, and the conversation with the children ended with why our font would be the only element from the sanctuary to go with us into the narthex—the promises of baptism are what ultimately hinge our community.

When we moved into the narthex, preaching, reading, confessions, and bible readings happened from the font. Our children's sermons involved filling the font with water, and I encouraged the children to splash members of the congregation at the end of the children's sermons. We began to refer to the front rows around the font as the "splash zone." I intentionally focused children's sermons on water themes in the lectionary (Noah's ark, Elisha crossing the Jordan, etc.), as I meant this new practice to be a temporary while we were worshiping outside of the historic sanctuary.

After two weeks everyone became accustomed to this practice; the children looked forward to the tactile experience of the water, and the congregation began to understand what we were doing, since we had practiced a baptismal rededication only a few weeks before. Our construction project ended and we were glad to return to the sanctuary, clean and bright with fresh new walls, refinished windows, and a completely repainted balcony.

What I did not expect when we returned to the renovated sanctuary was that when I invited the children to come forward for the first children's sermon in the new worship space, they did not come and sit down where we used to sit for our children's times, but they all returned to the font. They all came to the font and expected to touch water; I had not prepared for this and we had no water. (Luckily, though, I had some bottled water in the pulpit!) I had expected to go back to church as normal, but the experience of rededicating the adults' baptisms and teaching the children about our theological and spiritual connectedness to water actually adhered with the entire community. *Water is, after all, a physical and spiritual adhesive.*

Children's sermons are now practiced around the font, and we rededicate our baptisms informally every week. Not only has this become an integral part of our worship, but children often lead special liturgical rites from the font. Baptisms occur during the children's time: the children (whether they are baptized or not) bless the waters with their hands and lay their hands on the baby being baptized. The children do similar blessings when a member is moving away or leaving for college or celebrating the beginning or ending of the school year with our church school teachers. Now that water has become a central element of our public worship, our children have led us into new dimensions with our ritual practice.

The following Advent, our congregation again had a baptismal rededication service. The first time we did a baptismal rededication service, I invited our timid adults to come forward and receive a blessing with water, similar to an anointing with oil, or the ash ceremony for Ash Wednesday—except with water. The second time we did a baptismal rededication, *the children led the worship*: individual adults came forward, but the children laid their wet hands on the adults while I helped lead the prayers. We had a few visitors to church that day with children, and after the first few adults came forward, the non-churched children quickly caught on what they were supposed to do. This element of young flesh (New Flesh) touching the adults in a blessing is obviously pan-generational, but it connects the empathic nature of baptism across generations in the life cycle. Teaching children to lead worship helps them to liturgically habituate Christianity; children understand their role as blessings and leaders in the congregation.

Using water as a spiritual adhesive and tool for liturgical habituation can move in many new and different directions. One practice from another faith tradition that Christians may easily appropriate is Water Communion, a ritual I have borrowed from our Unitarian-Universalist cousins. For Unitarian-Universalists, Water Communion is often practiced on Rally Day, which is the day that Sunday school children are promoted and the church commences the religious education year. In preparation, at the end of springtime I distributed small plastic containers to children and adults to collect water from their travels over the summer—whether from their home, a grandparent's home, a vacation, camping trip, or a local creek. On Rally Day the children celebrated the water communion by collecting everyone's water and mixing it together in the font, and had a short discussion about the scarcity of clean water. I also invited a professor from the local college, who briefly spoke and poured some water from the Ganges River in India into the font. At the end of the worship service, I invited the adults to take the water to a grave of a loved one in our cemetery to return the water to the ground as a symbol of our enduring baptismal promises and the rest of the water was received into the earth at the grave of our congregation's founder.

In this congregation I have also learned to use the font for weddings, funerals, and other rites of the church, such as a corporate reconciliation service. Consequently the font leads the pan-generational community to invite children into leadership in these rituals which are often regarded as primarily for adults. Using water from the font at graveside committal services is particularly moving for all involved, especially when I may connect that the recently deceased was baptized, confirmed, married in the covenantal waters of the font. Not coincidentally, the children of the deceased often have connections to the font. The church records are thus employed liturgically for the purpose of pan-generational empathy. Baptism is what ecclesiastically connects us together.

We can largely predict future attitudes of children toward church by taking a hard look at where and how we spatially locate them in our facilities. For example, if we teach children to *leave* church for Sunday school, we essentially teach them that the sanctuary is adult space and the Education Wing is the kids' space. By simply opening access to the font the children reclaimed it as their own space and lead us in worship from the site of our initial sacrament. The children were teaching us, and especially me, what St. Augustine said when we wrote that the font is the womb of the church, a belief that we now weekly celebrate as an essential component of our worship life in our little country church. The font is a site for pan-generational ministry where we are led to live liturgically.

Religious Education
as Subversive Pastoral Ministry

Throughout this book we have explored the notion that feelings are rooted in a physiological configuration of our brains. Left to our own devices, we naturally retreat into solipsistic, individualized states that stiffly ritualize our behaviors and limit us from being open to new experiences and people. The good news is, however, that we can rise above these states and empathically enter into faith communities with others. We can, with practice and effort, acknowledge our dependence upon others at all points in our lives, against the common delusion that we are truly able to go it alone. To do this requires a long-term commitment to neurologically and habitually rewiring and being re-wired; to habituate into communities that are circles of empathy is a culturally *transgressive* activity.[33] It is to unlearn the *lie* that society, popular culture, Western economic and government systems, the American educational system, and even churches—and *especially* many youth ministries—teach us, namely, that our true self-actualization only requires ourselves.[34]

This is the *subversive* conclusion of this study. The way in which religious education is often delivered in American churches is decidedly a means by which the faith of young Christians is dismantled and killed—even while the reasons why many churches place a heavy emphasis upon the indoctrination of children and youth is to prevent them from leaving the church. So often we ask ourselves why teenagers leave the church when they are confirmed, while the way by which we have theologically defined the rite of confirmation is essentially a graduation from church: we often unknowingly give youth no other choice than to leave.

To this end, as a means of reversing these trends, I believe that there is no more truly subversive activity in our culture than genuine Christian ministry. But we must acknowledge that Christianity, as exemplified by mainstream youth ministry and religious education practices, has been diluted for generations of Americans. For many American Christians, to be "Christian" means to subscribe to a particular political party, to consume certain "Christian" products, and participate in church-based practices which often constitute an elaborate way of patting the white middle class on the back. For generations, to be "Christian" is simply to "check in" on Sunday mornings, or at least on Easter and Christmas, and "check out" the rest of the church year—the remainder of the year is simply *ordinary time*. Very often, ordinary time is filled with committee meetings. Aside from the nihilism implied by this current situation, we must acknowledge that the Christianity often practiced around us is a distant, far cry from anything authentically Christian or even remotely Biblical.

A popular cliché often stated in our culture is "education is the key." *Religious education* is the solution to the decrepit and torpid state of the contemporary church. The church needs to be re-educated, even while the church often functions as an institution interested in de-educating its believers about its own history, traditions, scriptures, and beliefs. The field of religious education, while it is being *weakened*, de-professionalized, and marginalized by churches and seminaries today is more essential than ever. Religious educators need to break out of the "education wings" of church buildings and take on new forms if the Christian faith is to again become relevant in our current situation.

Ritual is one necessary means by which the church may be re-educated and the faith be taught to all generations, especially the young. Demonstrating the necessity of empathy and pan-generational community within liturgical environments teaches the liturgical participants to *live* and *think liturgically*, to enact the ritual elements of the worship space into the worship space that is the banality of the world itself. If Christian worship is truly *extraordinary*, the ordinariness of life beyond the weekly hour spent in pan-generational worship will become transfigured into something truly New, *extra*-ordinary. Too often "newness" in Christian worship and religious education is simply a re-labeling of the old. The Christian faith, if it is to continue in the future in a vital and relevant way, looks not forward to something just *new*, but rather we stand in the hope of a faith extra-ordinarily New: "Behold, I am making all things new" (Rev. 21:5). We must Newly decide to follow Jesus—the Christ who was dis-membered and who, in ritual, we re-member—and believe that doing so leads us to live in Extraordinary Time.

This is Good News, especially for small churches. Many of us who minister within small church contexts catch ourselves enviously looking at large churches with expensive and complicated programs for children. Even if our churches could afford such programs, many of our churches do not have enough children to make these programs work or be worthwhile. Some of us have even given up on religious education programs because of our size and small numbers of participants. Conversely, we must recognize the extraordinary opportunity afforded to us in small churches to become liturgical sites for empathic pan-generational ministry. The small size of a church allows intimate sharing of emotion during worship and small churches tend to have a much *thinner* barrier already constructed between the church and our lives outside of the hour spent together on Sunday mornings. My point is to encourage those of us who minister in small churches or faith communities that extraordinary ministry is not only *essential* and *possible*, but it is *practical*, as well.

Regardless of our specific church contexts, the Good News is that for all of us, our Christian faith has a future. We must now actualize this future for ourselves.

NOTES: CHAPTER SIX

1. Cf. Rouget, 172ff; Freeman, (2000) 413.

2. David White, *Practicing Discernment With Youth* (Cleveland: Pilgrim, 2005), 208.

3. Cf. Katherine Turpin, *Branded* (Cleveland: Pilgrim, 2006), 212ff.

4. Mark DeVries, *Family-Based Youth Ministry*, rev. ed. (Downers Grove, IL: InterVarsity, 2006), 194-196.

5. Cf. Leonora Tisdale, *Preaching as Local Theology and Folk Art* (Minneapolis: Fortress, 1997), esp. 93ff.

6. Tom Beauchamp and James Childress, *Principles of Biomedical Ethics*, 5th ed. (New York: Oxford UP, 2001). In my view, Principlism in ethics has its antecedent in W. D. Ross' 1930 ethical masterpiece, *The Right and the Good* (London: Oxford UP, 1930).

7. There are many critiques of principlism, but I am particularly fond of Thomas Magnell's, which are found in two essays: "Fundamental and Technical Methods of Ethics," *International Journal of Value-Based Management* 9 (1996): 89-100; and "Harvard Ethics Consortium Case: The Burden of Moral Decision in Traumatic Treatment," *The Journal of Value Inquiry* 36 (2002): 553-547.

8. Adele Ahlberg Calhoun's *Spiritual Disciplines Handbook* (Downers Grove, IL: InterVarsity, 2005) is an excellent text for exploring traditional spiritual practices and rousing them in new ways. *Blessing New Voices* by Maren Tirabassi (Cleveland: Pilgrim, 2000) is a worthwhile starting point for examples of liturgy-making by teens. *For All the Saints*, ed. Clifton Guthrie (Akron, OH: OSL, 1995) is a great resource for developing a non-Catholic saint calendar. I use the 1979 version of the Episcopal Church's *The Common Book of Prayer*.

9. I use *The Book of Offices and Services After the Usage of the Order of Saint Luke*, 3rd ed. (Akron, OH: Order of Saint Luke, 1994).

10. Cf. Taylor W. Burton-Edwards, "From the Table, into the World," *Sacramental Life* 19 (Winter 2005-2006): 4-11.

11. One of the best resources for re-thinking Confirmation programs is Elizabeth Caldwell's *Leaving Home With Faith* (Cleveland: Pilgrim, 2002). Others worthy of mention include Peter Monkres and R. Kenneth Ostermiller, *The Rite of Confirmation* (Cleveland: United Church Press, 1995) and *Becoming & Belonging*, ed. by William Myers (Cleveland: United Church Press, 1993).

12. I have found Theodor Gaster's *Festivals of the Jewish Year* (New York: Morrow, 1952) a good guide for walking through the Jewish liturgical calendar. For Yom HaShoah, I have sponsored a film series or book discussions for youth—which included, coincidentally, the film, *The Seventh Chamber of Edith Stein* and Art Spiegelman's *Maus* Pulitzer Prize-winning graphic novels.

13. I use J. T. Waldman's *Megillat Esther* (Philadelphia, PA: Jewish Publication Society, 2005)—a comic book-like presentation of Esther in both Hebrew and contemporary English—or Eugene Peterson's Bible translation, *The Message* (2003).

14. Cf. Fred Edie, "Cultivating Baptismal Spirituality in High School Youth," *Doxology* 19 (2002): 85-107.

15. Julie Tallard Johnson's *Spiritual Journaling* (Rochester, VT: Bindu, 2006) is a good resource that I use for this practice.

16. As shown in Makanah Morriss et al, *Sexuality and Our Faith, A Companion to Our Whole Lives, Grades 7-9* and *10-12* (Boston: Unitarian Universalist Association/United Church Board of Homeland Ministries, 1999 and 2000).

17. Julie Tallard Johnson's *I Ching for Teens* (Rochester, VT: Bindu, 2001) and M. J. Abadie's *Tarot for Teens* (Rochester, VT: Bindu, 2002) are good resources—which need some interpretation for use in Christian communities—for these practices. For a theoretical foundation of integrating these practices, see Marinoff (*Plato, Not Prozac!* [New York: Quill, 2000], esp. 301ff.) and Goldenberg, 100-101.

18. Marjorie Corbman, *A Tiny Step Away From Deepest Faith* (Brewster, Mass.: Paraclete, 2005).

19. I use Michael Caduto and Joseph Bruchac's *Keepers of the Animals* (Golden, CO: Fulcrum, 1991), a collection of stories from the Native American traditions for children; and a resource that the local Order of the Arrow lodge has distributed in a local Boy Scout camp (*Religious Services for Mornings and Evenings*, rev. ed., comp. Robert Mason).

20. Freeman (1997), 69. Pilgrim Press' *Making Liturgy: Creating Rituals for Worship and Life* (ed. Dorothea McEwan et al) and Vanessa Ochs' *Inventing Jewish Ritual* are good guides for creating new and reclaiming old practices and traditions (Dorothy McEwan, Pat Pinsent, Ianthe Pratt, and Veronica Seddon, eds., *Making Liturgy* [Cleveland: Pilgrim, 2001]; Ochs, *Inventing Jewish Ritual* [Philadelphia: Jewish Publication Society, 2007]). Dori Grinenko Baker's *Doing Girlfriend Theology* (Cleveland: Pilgrim, 2005) is a fantastic resource for launching feminist story groups

with girls. Dorothy Bass and Don Richter's (eds.) *Way to Live* (Nashville: Upper Room, 2002) is a good book for younger youth to launch discussions about liturgical living. For older youth or college students, use Tony Jones' *Soul Shaper* (El Cajon, CA: Youth Specialties/Zondervan, 2003). Daniel Erlander's excellent illustrated books—*Mana and Mercy* (Mercer Island, WA: Order of Saints Martin and Teresa, 1992), *Let the Children Come* (D. Erlander, 1996), and *A Place for You*—are fantastic resources for baptism, confirmation, and first communion with young people or college students as well.

21. Cf. George Williams, *The Radical Reformation* (Philadelphia: Westminster, 1962), 472ff.

22. Dan O'Keefe, *The Real Festivus* (New York: Perigee, 2005), esp. 84-85.

23. In case anyone wishes to argue, as some have with my position, there is scriptural and historical basis for *poaching* scriptures to invent new rituals. For examples, see Ignatius Hunt's excellent *The Bible and Liturgy* (Glen Rock, NJ: Paulist, 1963), esp. 13-18. Incidentally, Hunt's analysis of the biblical foundations for Christian worship in this short little book is, in my opinion, unparalleled.

24. Cf. Caldwell 47-66; Kenda Creasy Dean and Ron Foster, *The Godbearing Life* (Nashville: Upper Room, 1998), esp. 89-102; Roberta and Christopher Nelson, *Parents as Spiritual Guides* (Boston, MA: Unitarian Universalist, 2001).

25. Csikszentmihalyi writes of an example of a child who was forced to go to classical music concerts with his parents. Later, the man recalls disliking the experience, but after some time he experienced "an ecstatic insight," that is, "he suddenly discovered the melodic structure of the [classical music] piece, and had an overwhelming sense of a new world opening up before him." Continuing: "It was *three years* of *painful listening* that had prepared him for this epiphany.... Of course, he was lucky; many children never reach the point of recognizing the possibilities of the activity into which they are forced, and end up disliking it forever" (Csikszentmihalyi 68, emph. add.). Csikszentmihalyi summarizes, "[s]ome things we are initially forced to do against our will turn out in the course of time to be intrinsically rewarding" (67).

26. "Jesus, Remember Me": from *The United Methodist Hymnal*. 1989 ed. (Nashville: United Methodist, 1989), no. 488.

27. Karl Rahner, *Encounters With Silence* (South Bend, IN: St. Augustine's, 1999), 86, 87.

28. This theological focus is, not coincidentally, a central theme in Rahner's theological writing. For Rahner, theologically stated, the Christian definition of death as *not* non-being is, from my reading of Rahner, the starting point for declaring the content of Christian reality.

29. This ritual was previously published in Christopher Rodkey, "Turning Away from Our Dead," *Sacramental Life* 17.3 (2005): 12-14. A similar ritual and perspective may be found in Brett Webb-Mitchell and Diane Archer's *Sacred Seasons* (Cleveland: Pilgrim, 2002), 99-103.

30. See, for example, *The United Methodist Book of Worship* (Nashville: UMC, 1992), 437-439.

31. Cf. Mary Daly, *Beyond God The Father: Toward a Philosophy of Women's Liberation* (Boston: Beacon, 1973), 145-146; Mary Daly and Jane Caputi, 86.

32. This conversation was previously published, with additional commentary, in Christopher Rodkey, "A Polemic Against the 'Festival of the Christian Home.'"

33. Cf. bell hooks, *Teaching to Transgress* (New York: Routledge, 1994); Mandler, 28-29.

34. Cf. Michael Warren, *Youth Gospel Liberation* (Dublin: Veritas, 1998).

Selected Bibliography

Andrews, Michael. *Contributions to the Phenomenology of Empathy*. Ph.D. dissertation, Villanova University (Villanova, PA), 2002.
Barnes, Brian. *Versions of Empathy*. M.A. thesis, University of Louisville (KY), 1997.
Bataille, Georges. *Erotism.* Trans. Mary Dalwood. San Francisco: City Lights, 1975.
Beauchamp, Tom, and James Childress. *Principles of Biomedical Ethics.* 5th ed. New York: Oxford UP, 2001.
Bell, Catherine. *Ritual Theory, Ritual Practice.* New York: Oxford UP, 1992.
Bello, Angela. "Edith Stein's Contribution to Phenomenology." *Phenomenology World-Wide.* Dordrecht, The Netherlands: Kluwer, 2002. 232-240.
Benzon, William. *Beethoven's Anvil.* New York: Basic, 2001.
Bliss, T., and T. Lømo. "Long-Lasting Potentiation of Synaptic Transmission in the Dentate Area of the Anaesthetized Rabbit Following Stimulation of the Perforant Path." *Journal of Physiology* 232 (1973): 331-356.
Bourdieu, Pierre. *Outline of a Theory of Practice.* Trans. Richard Nice. Cambridge, England: Cambridge UP, 1977.
Brown, Delwin. *Boundaries of our Habituations.* Albany, NY: SUNY, 1994.
Brown, James. "Faith, Flesh and Feeling." *Worship* 60.3 (2001): 225-231.
Buller, David. *Adapting Minds.* Cambridge, MA: MIT UP, 2005.
Churchland, Patricia. *Brain-Wise.* Cambridge, MA: MIT UP, 2002.
Corrigan, John. "Introduction." *Religion and Emotion: Approaches and Interpretations.* Ed. John Corrigan. New York: Oxford UP, 2004. 3-31.
Csikszentmihalyi, Mihaly. *Flow.* Grand Rapids, MI: Harper, 1990.
d'Aquili, Eugene, and Andrew Newberg. *The Mystical Mind.* Minneapolis: Fortress, 1999.
d'Aquili, Eugene, Andrew Newberg, and Vince Rouse. *Why God Won't Go Away.* New York: Ballantine, 2001.
Depraz, Natalie. "The Husserlian Theory of Intersubjectivity as Alteriology: Emergent Theories and Wisdom Traditions in Light of Genetic Phenomenology." *Journal of Consciousness Studies* 8:5-7 (2001): 169-168.
Damasio, Antonio. *Looking for Spinoza.* Orlando, FL: Harcourt, 2003.
Dolan, Raymond and John Morris. "The Functional Anatomy of Innate and Acquired Fear: Perspectives from Neuro-imaging." *Cognitive Neuroscience of Emotion.* Ed. Richard Lane and Lynn Nadel. New York: Oxford UP, 2000. 225-241.

Edwards, Jonathan. *Thoughts on the Revival of Religion in New England, 1740.* Worchester ed. New York: American Tract Society, 1845.
Feit, Allison. *Implicit Affect.* Ph.D. dissertation, Adelphi University (Garden City, NY), 2005.
Feit, Jonathan. "Probing Neurotheology's Brain, or Critiquing an Emerging Quasi-Science." *The Council of Societies for the Study of Religion Bulletin* 33.1 (Feb. 2004): 3-9.
Felts, Elizabeth, and Anthony Robinson. *New Occasions Teach New Duties.* Cleveland, OH: United Church of Christ Division of Education and Publication, 1994.
Fredrickson, Barbara. "Gratitude, Like Other Positive Emotions, Broadens and Builds." *The Psychology of Gratitude.* Ed. Robert Emmons and Michael McCullough. New York: Oxford UP, 2004. 145-166.
Freeman, Walter. "A Neurological Role of Music in Social Bonding." *The Origins of Music.* Ed. Nils Wallin, Björn Merker, and Steven Brown. Cambridge, MA: MIT UP, 2000.
———. "Happiness Doesn't Come in Bottles: Neuroscientists Learn that Joy Comes through Dancing, Not Drugs." *Journal of Consciousness Studies* 4.1 (1997): 67-70.
———. *Societies of Brains.* Hillsdale, NJ: Lawrence Erlbaum, 1995.
Gorday, Peter. *Empathic Knowing and Mystical Knowing.* M.Th. thesis, Columbia Theological Seminary (Decatur, GA), 1995.
Hebb, D. "Emotion in Man and Animal: An Analysis of the Intuitive Processes of Recognition." *Psychological Review* 53 (1946): 88-106.
———. *The Organization of Behavior.* New York: Wiley, 1949.
Hogue, David. *Remembering the Future, Imagining the Past.* Cleveland: Pilgrim, 2003.
Husserl, Edmund. *The Essential Husserl.* Ed. Donn Welton. Bloomington, IN: Indiana UP, 1999.
———. *Ideas Pertaining to a Pure Phenomenological Philosophy, Second Book: Studies in the Phenomenology of Constitution.* Trans. Richard Rojcewicz and André Schuwer. Edmund Husserl: Collected Works. Vol. 3. Dordrecht, The Netherlands: Kluwer, 1989.
Kandel, Eric. "Biology and the Future of Psychoanalysis: A New Intellectual Framework for Psychiatry Revisited." *American Journal of Psychiatry* 156.4 (April 1999): 505-524.
———. *Cellular Basis of Behavior.* San Francisco: Freeman, 1976.
———. "Genes, Nerve Cells, and the Remembrance of Things Past." *Journal of Neuropsychiatry* 1.2 (1999):103-125.
———. "Genes, Synapses, and Long-Term Memory." *Journal of Cellular Physiology* 173 (1997): 124-125.
———. "A New Intellectual Framework for Psychiatry." *American Journal of Psychiatry* 155.4 (April 1998): 457-469.
Kandel, Eric, and Christopher Pittenger. "The Past, the Future, and the Biology of Memory Storage." *Philosophical Trans. of the Royal Society of London B* 354 (1999): 2027-2052.
Kandel, Eric, and James Schwartz. "Molecular Biology of Learning: Modulation of Transmitter Release." *Science* 218 (29. Oct. 1982): 433-443.
Kavanagh, Aidan. *On Liturgical Theology.* Collegeville, MN: Liturgical Press, 1992.
Kim, Jeansok, and Mark Baxter. "Multiple Brain-Memory Systems: The Whole Does Not Equal the Sum of Its Parts." *Trends in Neuroscience* 24.6 (June 2001): 324-330.
Kohut, Heinz. *The Analysis of the Self.* Madison, CT: International Universities, 1971.

———. *The Chicago Institute Lectures.* Ed. Paul Tolpin. Hillsdale, IL: Analytic, 1996.
———. *How Does Analysis Cure?* Ed. Arnold Goldberg and Paul Stepansky. Chicago: U Chicago P, 1984.
———. *The Psychology of the Self: A Casebook.* Ed. Arnold Goldberg et al. Madison, CT: International Universities, 1978.
Konorski, Jerzy. *Conditional Reflexes and Neuron Organization.* 1968 ed. Trans. Stephen Garry. New York: Hafner, 1968.
LeDoux, Joseph. *The Emotional Brain.* New York: Touchtone, 1996.
———. *Synaptic Self.* New York: Penguin, 2002.
Lipps., T. *Leitfaden der Psychologie.* Leipsig: Engelmann, 1909.
Magnell, Thomas. "Fundamental and Technical Methods of Ethics." *International Journal of Value-Based Management* 9 (1996): 89-100.
———. "Harvard Ethics Consortium Case: The Burden of Moral Decision in Traumatic Treatment." *The Journal of Value Inquiry* 36 (2002): 553-547.
Maslow, Abraham. *The Farther Reaches of Human Nature.* New York: Viking, 1971.
———. *Motivation and Personality.* 2nd ed. Ed. Wayne Holtzman and Gardner Murphy. New York: Harper, 1970.
———. *Toward a Psychology of Being.* 2nd ed. New York: Van Nostrand Reinhold, 1968.
McAdams, Dan, and Jack Bauer. "Gratitude in Modern Life: Its Manifestations and Development." *The Psychology of Gratitude.* Ed. Robert Emmons and Michael McCullough. New York: Oxford UP, 2004. 81-99.
McCraty, Rollin, and Doc Childre. "The Grateful Heart: The Psychophysiology of Appreciation." *The Psychology of Gratitude.* Ed. Robert Emmons and Michael McCullough. New York: Oxford UP, 2004. 230-255.
Newberg, Andrew, and Jeremy Iverson. "On the 'Neuro' in Neurotheology." *NeuroTheology.* Ed. R. Joseph. San Jose, CA: University, Press, 2003. 251-269.
Ornstein, Robert. *The Psychology of Consciousness.* San Francisco: Freeman, 1972.
Panksepp, Jaak. *Affective Neuroscience.* Oxford: Oxford UP, 1998.
———. "The Emotional Sources of 'Chills' Induced by Music." *Music Perception* 13.2 (1995): 171-207.
Panzarella, Robert. "The Phenomenology of Aesthetic Peak Experiences." *Journal of Humanistic Psychology* 20.1 (1980): 69-85.
Rahner, Karl. *Encounters With Silence.* South Bend, IN: St. Augustine's, 1999.
Ricoeur, Paul. "The Question of Proof in Freud's Psychoanalytic Writings." *Journal of the American Psychoanalytic Association* 25 (1977) 835-871.
Ricoeur, Paul, and André LaCocque. *Thinking Biblically.* Trans. David Pellauer. Chicago: U Chicago P, 1998.
Roberts, Robert, and W. Wood. "Proper Function, Emotion, and Virtues of the Intellect." *Faith and Philosophy* 21.1 (Jan. 2004): 3-24.
Rodkey, Christopher. "A Polemic Against 'The Festival of the Christian Home.'" *Sacramental Life* 17.2 (2005): 18-23.
———. "The Children's Sermon as Liturgical Movement." *Education in the Church* (October, 2009), online.
———. "The Practice of Music in Youth Ministry and the Mystery of the Divine." *Journal of Youth and Theology* 5.2 (2006): 47-62.
———. "Reality Check: Confirmation *is* Graduation." *The Education Connection* (Winter, 2008) 4+.
———. "Reconsidering Noise in Theology and in Praxis." *Doxology* 21 (2004): 72-91.

———. Review of *Human Experience* by John Russon. *Philosophical Practice* 2.1 (2006): 61-63.
———. "Teach to Provoke!" *YouthWorker Journal* 22.6 (July/Aug., 2006): 48-49.
———. "Turning Away from Our Dead." *Sacramental Life* 17.2 (2005): 7-9
Ross, W. *The Right and the Good*. London: Oxford UP, 1930.
Russon, John. *Human Experience*. Albany, NY: SUNY UP, 2003.
Schleiermacher, Friedrich. *Christian Caring: Selections from Practical Theology*. Trans. James Duke. Ed. James Duke and Howard Stone. Minneapolis: Fortress, 1988.
———. *The Christian Faith*. 2nd German Ed. Ed. H. Mackintosh and J. Stewart. Edinburgh: T & T, 1952.
Shatz, Carla. "Dividing Up the Neocortex." *Science* 258.5080 (9. Oct. 1992): 237(2).
———. "Emergence of Order in Visual System Development." *Proceedings of the National Academy of Sciences USA* 93 (Jan. 1996): 602-608.
Smith, David. *The Circle of Acquaintance*. Dordrecht, The Netherlands: Kluwer, 1989.
Stein, Edith. *Essential Writings*. Ed. John Sullivan. Maryknoll, NY: Orbis, 2002.
———. *On the Problem of Empathy*. 3rd rev. ed. Trans. Waltraut Stein. The Collected Works of Edith Stein. Vol. 3. Washington, DC: ICS, 1989.
———. *Selected Writings*. Trans. Susanne Baltzdorff. Springfield, IL: 1990.
Stryker, Michael. "Activity-Dependent Reorganization of Afferents in the Developing Mammalian Visual System." *Development of the Visual System*. Ed. Dominic Lam and Carla Shatz. Cambridge, MA: MIT UP, 1991. 267-287.
Thandeka. *The Embodied Self*. Albany, NY: SUNY UP, 1995.
———. "Schleiermacher's *Affekt* Theology." *International Journal of Pastoral Theology* 9 (2005): 197-216.
Thompson, Evan. "Empathy and Consciousness" *Journal of Consciousness Studies* 8:5-7 (2001): 1-32.
Tononi, Giulio, and Gerald Edelman. "Consciousness and Complexity." *Essential Sources in the Scientific Study of Consciousness*. Ed. Bernard Baurs, William Bowls, and James Newman. Cambridge, MA: MIT UP, 2003. 993-1005.
Watkins, Philip. "Gratitude and Subjective Well-Being." *The Psychology of Gratitude*. Ed. Robert Emmons and Michael McCullough. New York: Oxford UP, 2004. 167-192.
Wesley, John, and Charles Wesley. *Selected Writings and Hymns*. Ed. Frank Whaling. New York: Paulist, 1981.
White, James. *Intergenerational Religious Education*. Birmingham, AL: Religious Education Press, 1988.
Williams, Forrest. "Intersubjectivity: A Brief Guide." *Husserl's Phenomenology: A Textbook*. Ed. J. Mohanty and William McKenna. Washington, DC: Center for Advanced Phenomenology and University Press of America, 1989. 309-343.
Winnicott, D. *Playing and Reality*. London: Tavistock/Roudtledge, 1991.
Zahavi, Dan. "Beyond Empathy: Phenomenological Approaches to Intersubjectivity." *Journal of Consciousness Studies* 8:5-7 (2001): 151-167.

Index

Adult development, 30, 36, 63
Affect theology, 8, 11n
All Saints' Sunday, 77-79
Altizer, Thomas, v, 2, 8n
Andrews, Michael, 18
Aristotle, 52-53, 55
Ascension Day, 76
Autotelic experience, 37, 38, 70

Baptism, 23, 58, 68, 75, 76, 78, 79, 81-83
Bauer, Jack, 51, 59n
Baxter, Mark, 28, 29
Beauchamp, Tom, 74
Being-at-home, 55
Being-somewhere, 17
Being-with-others, 18, 24-25n
Bell, Catherine, 50
Benzon, William, 30-31, 57-58
Bio-medical ethics, 74
Birth, 23
Bliss, T., 28
Blood pressure, 27
Bodily fluids, 27
Bourdieu, Pierre, 54
Bowrey El effect, 53-54
Brain, 1, 2-3, 6, 24, 27-39, 52, 67, 71n

Candler School of Theology, v
Catechisms, 73, 81
Cerebral cortex, 31

Chalice lightings, 76
Child development, childhood, 30, 56, 63
Childre, Doc, 50-51
Children's ministry, 73, 81-83, 85, 86-87n
Children's sermons, 63, 76, 81-83
Childress, James, 74
Churchland, Patricia, 29-30, 41n
Circle of perception, 21
Civic holidays, 69
Clarity, phenomenological, 19, 22
Co-existence, 14, 15
Collusion, 14, 15
Common Book of Prayer, 75
Community Church (Mountain Lakes, NJ), *v-vi*
Community, 21-24, 39, 58, 67, 70, 74, 80, 83
Confirmation, 66, 68, 75, 76, 83, 86n
Congregationalism, 4
Con-primordiality, 21
Contemporary Christian Music, 5, 6, 10n
Context-sensitivity, 32
Continental philosophy, 4, 13
Co-presence, 15, 16, 17, 24-25n
Corbman, Margorie, 76
Corrigan, John, 3
Creeds, 57, 73
Csikszentmihalyi, Mihaly, 37, 38, 71n,

87n

Daly, Mary, 9n, 88n
d'Aquili, Eugene, 34-35, 44-45n, 61n
Deep penetration, epistemic, 14-15, 16-17
The Deer Hunter, 49
Demasio, Antonio, 32, 43n, 44n
Dendrites, 28-29, 31, 60n
Depraz, Natalie, 17
Descartes, René, 17, 35, 45n
Determinancy, 54-55
Developmental plasticity, 30-32
DeVries, Mark, 74
Digestion, phenomenological, 20
Dilthey, William, 19
Dis-habituation, 55
Disney World, 50
Drumming, 73

Ecstasy, 37
Edelman, Gerald, 32-33
Edwards, Jonathan, 4
Eeyore, 51
Ego-subject, 16
Embodiment, 8
Emergence Christianity, 6, 10n
Emotion, 1n, 2, 3, 4, 9n, 27-39, 44n, 50-52, 68
Emotional value operator, 34
Empathy (*Einfühlung*), 3-4, 13-24, 52, 67, 74, 77, 79, 83
Enfleshment, 8
Epistemology, 3
Esoterism, Western, 68
Essentialism, 3
Ethics, 17, 52-53, 74
Eucharist, 56, 65-66, 75-76
Existential operator, 34-35, 44n
Extraordinariness, Extraordinary Time, 84-85

Father's Day, 69, 80
Feeling (*Gefühl*), 1-2, 3-4, 7-8, 14-16, 19, 20, 21-23, 27-39, 44n, 45n, 49
Felts, Elizabeth, 63-64, 71n
Feminism, 72n, 80
Festival of the Christian Home, 72n, 79-80
Festivus, 77

Film, 39, 49, 51
Flow experience, 37, 38
Foot washing, 76
Fraser, Jill, 67
Fredrickson, Barbara, 51, 52
Freeman, Walter, 57, 58, 60n, 67, 71n
Freemasonry, 23, 68
Funerals, burial rituals, 23, 52, 56-57

Gabrielson, Alf, 37
Gastrointestinal motility, 27
German Idealism, 7
Gorday, Peter, 19
Group emotions, 51-52

Habituation, 7, 8, 29, 31, 32, 33-37, 43n, 50-58, 63, 65, 68, 69, 70, 73, 77, 79, 82
Hebb, D., 28-30, 41n
Heidelberg Catechism, 81
Hermeneutic lens, 34
Hippocampus, 43-44n
Hippocratic oath, 74
Hogue, David, 9n, 70
Hooks, Bell, 88n
Hume, David, 3
Husserl, Edmund, 3, 14-23, 24-25n, 26n
Hutcheson, Francis, 3
Hybridity, religious, 4

I Ching, 76, 86n
I, *I-ness*, 7-8, 14-15, 16, 17, 19-21, 35, 55
Imitation, 20, 23, 58
Infant development, infancy, 30, 32, 52
Initiation, 75
Inter-generational religious education, 65n
Intersubjectivity, 17
Intimacy, 22

Judaism, 76, 86-87n

Kalinnikov, V., 39
Kandel, Eric, 28-29, 42n, 43-44n, 53
Kavanagh, Aidan, 58
Kim, Jeansok, 28, 29
Kingdom of God, 2, 8, 70
Kohut, Heinz, 13-14, 22

Index

Konorski, Jerzy, 28

Labor Day, 80
Ladies' Aid Societies, 81
Language, phenomenology of, 16, 36
Leader emotions, 52
Learning, 31, 32-33, 42n, 71n
LeDoux, Joseph, 31, 33, 41n, 47n
Liberation, 8, 36, 38, 55, 57, 67, 69, 79
Life cycle, 30, 56, 63, 68, 75, 77
Lipps, T., 13, 19
Liturgical ecology, 75-85
Liturgical perfuming, 56-57, 73
Liturgical seasons, 69, 76, 78, 81, 82, 84, 86n
Liturgical theology, 1, 6, 56, 68
Living liturgically, 8, 69-70, 73, 74, 77, 80, 84-85
Lømo, T., 28
Long-term potentiation, LTP, 33
Lord's Prayer, 57
Love Feasts, 76
Ludology, 70

Marching band, 39
Marinoff, Lou, 86n
Marriage, 23
Marriage, 23
Maslow, Abraham, 27
McAdams, Dan, 51, 59n
McCraty, Rollin, 50-51
Memorial Day, 69
Memorialization, 23
Memory, 20, 28, 30, 31, 32-33, 42n, 43n, 54, 68, 73
Milne, A., 51
Modulation, 32-33
Moods, 50-52
Moravians, 5
Mormons, 5
Mother's Day, 69, 79-80
Music, 10n, 37-39, 47n, 56, 57, 60n, 61n, 71n, 73, 87n

Native American spirituality, 76, 86n
Natural philosophy, 3
Nature hikes, 76
Neurology, 1, 7, 8-9n, 27-39, 53, 56, 57-58, 63, 69, 73, 74, 77
Neuro-modulary cholinergic projections, 28
Neuro-peptide, 31, 57
Neuro-theology, 2-3, 8n, 47n
New Creation, 70, 85
Newberg, Andrew, 34-35, 44-45n, 61n
Not-me, 7-8

O'Keefe, Daniel, 77
Ontology, 27
Ornstein, Robert, 53-54
Orthodox Christianity, 68
Orthodoxy, 5
Other, otherness, 14-15, 16, 17, 18, 19-20, 52
Oxytocin, oxytoxin, 31-32, 57-58, 61n

Pan-generational religious education, 65, 73, 74, 77, 83, 85
Pangerl, Susann, v
Panksepp, Jaak, 8n, 35-36, 38, 42n, 45n, 55
Panzarella, Robert, 27
Papillary response, 27
The Passion of the Christ, 49
Peak experience, peaking, 37-39
Pedagogical abuse, 63
Perception, 20-21
Phenomenology, 14-22, 24n
Pittenger, Christopher, 28-29
Plasticity, neural, 28-33, 35-36, 38, 44n, 50, 69
Positivity, 50-52, 70
Post-developmental plasticity, 30-32
Post-synaptic change, 30, 42n, 43n
Potentiation, 33
Prayer, 13, 39, 56, 71n, 75, 78
Pre-natal plasticity, 41n
Pre-synaptic change, 30, 42n
Principlism, 74-75, 85-86n
Protestantism, 4, 5-6, 58, 76, 81
Psychoanalysis, 13
Psycho-physical, 19, 20
Puberty, 23
Purim, 76

Quakers, 76
Quasi-religious, 23

Radical Christianity, v, 2, 8n, 83-85
Radical Reformation, 76

Index

Rahner, Karl, 78, 87n
Rally Day, 82-83
Rebirth, 58
Reciprocation, 23, 28, 67
Reflection, 20
Reformation, 3
Regeneration, 8, 69
Reiterated empthy, 21
Religious education, 1, 52, 63-70
Repression, 54
Resurrection, 69
Ricoeur, Paul, 69
Rimsky-Korsakov, Nikolai, 39
Ritual, 23, 27, 31, 36, 38, 50, 55, 56-58, 61n, 68-70, 72n, 75-80, 83, 86-87n
Robinson, Anthony, 63-64, 71n
Roman Catholicism, 4, 5, 18, 51, 56-57, 61n, 68, 73
Rouse, Vince, 34-35, 44-45n
Russon, John, 50, 54-55

Sabbath observation, 69
Sacramental theology, 75-76
Scheler, Max, 19
Schleiermacher, Friedrich, 7-8, 11n
Schwenkfelders, 76
Scottish Enlightenment, 3
Scouting, 76, 86n
Secular order, 75
Seinfeld, 77
"SELF," 35-36, 45n, 54, 55
Self-actualization, 3, 37, 38, 56, 57, 58, 67, 68, 70, 85
Self-affirmation, 52
Selfishness, 17-18
Self-knowing, 3, 16-17
Self-projection, 21
Self-psychology, 14
Self-representation mechanism, 35-36
Seminaries, 6, 84
Sensus communis, 3
Service trips, 75
Shatz, Carla, 29
Shrinkage, phenomenological, 20
Skin, 27
Smith, David, 20-21
Snake-handling, 5
Solipsism, 17, 22, 24, 52, 83
Sphere of ownness, 14, 15, 16-17

Spirituality, spiritual disciplines, 1-2, 21, 69, 86n
Stein, Edith, 3, 14, 18-23, 26n, 86n
Story, storytelling, 56, 67, 68, 76
Structural transformation, 20-21
Stryker, Michael, 28
Subjectivity, 17, 54
Sunday Schools, 64-65, 71n, 82-83
Synapses, 28-30, 33, 57-58

Taboos, 68
Taizé worship, 78, 79
Tarot cards, 76, 86n
Teknik, 7
Television Evangelism, 5
Thalamo-amygdala and thalamo-cortio-amygdala pathways, 41n
Thandeka, v, 7, 11n, 45n
Theology, 19-20
Thereness-of-me, 15
Thinking Biblically, 69
Thinking liturgically, 8, 69-70, 74, 77, 84-85
Tononi, Guilio, 32-33
Trance state, 38

Unction, 23
Unitarian Universalism, 4, 82-83
United Church of Christ, v, 4, 63

Water Communion, 82-83
Watkins, Philip, 52
Wesleyanism, 4
Williams, Forrest, 17
Winnie-the-Pooh, 51
Worship, 1, 3, 4, 5-7, 10n, 13, 23, 49-58, 56-59, 63-70, 74, 77-79

Yom HaShoah, 76, 86n
Young adulthood, 56
Youth ministry, 13, 65-66, 73-85, 86-87n

Zahavi, Dan, 18
Zero-point, phenomenological, 21, 22, 26n

www.ingramcontent.com/pod-product-compliance
Lightning Source LLC
Chambersburg PA
CBHW070645300426
44111CB00013B/2271